BAPTISM

THREE VIEWS

EDITED BY David F. Wright

CONTRIBUTIONS BY Sinclair B. Ferguson, Anthony N. S. Lane and Bruce A. Ware

IVP Academic

An imprint of InterVarsity Press
Downers Grove, Illinois

InterVarsity Press
P.O. Box 1400, Downers Grove, IL 60515-1426
World Wide Web: www.ivpress.com
E-mail: email@ivpress.com

*InterVarsity Press® is the book-publishing division of InterVarsity Christian Fellowship/USA®, a movement
of students and faculty active on campus at hundreds of universities, colleges and schools of nursing in the
United States of America, and a member movement of the International Fellowship of Evangelical Students.
For information about local and regional activities, write Public Relations Dept., InterVarsity Christian
Fellowship/USA, 6400 Schroeder Rd., P.O. Box 7895, Madison, WI 53707-7895, or visit the IVCF
website at <www.intervarsity.org>.*

Design: Cindy Kiple
Images: Ryan McVay/Getty Images

ISBN 978-0-8308-3856-1

Printed in the United States of America ∞

Library of Congress Cataloging-in-Publication Data

*Baptism: three views/edited by David F. Wright; with contributions
by Sinclair B. Ferguson, Anthony N.S. Lane, and Bruce A. Ware.*
    p. cm.
  Includes bibliographical references and index.
  ISBN 978-0-8308-3856-1 (pbk.: alk. paper)
  *1. Baptism. I. Wright, David F. II. Ferguson, Sinclair B. III.
Lane, A. N. S. IV. Ware, Bruce A.*
  BV812.B37 2009
  234'.161—dc22
                          2009021518

| P | 21 | 20 | 19 | 18 | 17 | 16 | 15 | 14 | 13 | 12 | 11 | 10 | 9 | 8 | 7 | 6 | 5 | 4 | 3 | 2 |
| Y | 26 | 25 | 24 | 23 | 22 | 21 | 20 | 19 | 18 | 17 | 16 | 15 | 14 | 13 | 12 | 11 | 10 | 09 |

In Memoriam

David F. Wright

(1937-2008)

CONTENTS

ABBREVIATIONS

ACW   Ancient Christian Writers: The Works of the Fathers in Translation. Mahwah, N.J.: Paulist Press, 1946-.

AF   J. B. Lightfoot and J. R. Harmer, trans. *The Apostolic Fathers*. Edited by M. W. Holmes. 2nd ed. Grand Rapids: Baker, 1989.

ANF   A. Roberts and J. Donaldson, eds. Ante-Nicene Fathers. 10 vols. Buffalo, N.Y.: Christian Literature, 1885-1896. Reprint, Grand Rapids: Eerdmans, 1951-1956; Reprint, Peabody, Mass.: Hendrickson, 1994.

CCL   Corpus Christianorum. Series Latina. Turnhout, Belgium: Brepols, 1953-.

FC   Fathers of the Church: A New Translation. Washington, D.C.: Catholic University of America Press, 1947-.

LCC   J. Baillie et al., eds. The Library of Christian Classics. 26 vols. Philadelphia: Westminster Press, 1953-1966; Reprint, Louisville: Westminster John Knox Press.

NIDNTT Colin Brown, ed. *New International Dictionary of New Testament Theology*. 4 vols. Grand Rapids: Zondervan, 1986.

NPNF[1] P. Schaff et al., eds. A Select Library of the Nicene and Post-Nicene Fathers of the Christian Church. Series 1. 14 vols. Buffalo, N.Y.: Christian Literature, 1887-1894. Reprint, Grand Rapids: Eerdmans, 1952-1956. Reprint, Peabody, Mass.: Hendrickson, 1994.

NPNF[2]   P. Schaff et al., eds. A Select Library of the Nicene and
           Post-Nicene Fathers of the Christian Church. Series 2.
           14 vols. Buffalo, N.Y.: Christian Literature, 1887-1894.
           Reprint, Grand Rapids: Eerdmans, 1952-1956. Re-
           print, Peabody, Mass.: Hendrickson, 1994.

PG   J.-P. Migne, ed. Patrologia Graeca. 166 vols. Paris:
           Migne, 1857-1886.

PL   J.-P. Migne, ed. Patrologia Latina. 221 vols. Paris:
           Migne, 1844-1864.

SC   H. de Lubac, J. Daniélou et al., eds. Sources Chré-
           tiennes. Paris: Editions du Cerf, 1941-.

TDNT   Gerhard Kittel and Gerhard Friedrich, eds. *Theological
           Dictionary of the New Testament*. Translated by Geoffrey W.
           Bromiley. 10 vols. Grand Rapids: Eerdmans,
           1964-1976.

INTRODUCTION

Daniel G. Reid

As I prepared to write this introduction, I came across a news story about the dedication of a new baptismal font. The font is described and pictured as an object of stunning beauty, cruciform in shape, oriented on the four cardinal points of the compass, with its "living" water quietly gliding over the font's dark surface, reflecting the arched ceiling of the church. And it is large enough to accommodate baptism by immersion.

This font, located in the Anglican Cathedral in Salisbury, England, is the first permanent font to be installed in that cathedral in over a century. Its capacity for immersion might surprise some Baptists or even Presbyterians. Those who know their church history will recall that baptismal fonts of this size have an ancient history in the church, as evidenced in archaeological remains going back to the baptistery in the house church at Dura-Europas of the early third century. The Salisbury font, installed in this centuries-old cathedral, is a reminder of the sacred place of baptism in Christian practice, the beauty that it can inspire, the complexity of its history and, for some, the conflicted practice of baptism in the Anglican Church of post-Christendom.

While the Salisbury baptismal font evokes tranquility, baptismal waters are not always so! They have also inspired controversy and debate, and even some regrettable chapters in church history. We have all heard the advice not to bring up religion or politics at dinner parties. Too often these conversations do not end well. For those who are accustomed to discussing religion or theology among the mixed company of the faithful, perhaps the advice should be, "No discussing *baptism* or politics!" Baptism—its subjects, its relation to faith, its meaning and its mode of application—is a topic that the experienced have learned to sidestep to preserve the peace, certainly within the context of evangelical nondenominational parachurch movements.

The fact that in this book we have three theologians representing three different views gathered around the table to talk about baptism should be an attraction in itself. That we did not feel the need to remove any sharp cutlery from the table and that no fight erupts over these divisive waters is a tribute to their deeper recognition of the "one baptism" of which Paul spoke (Eph 4:5), even if that baptism is refracted through different forms and practices.

Karl Barth, who during his theological career changed his allegiance from paedobaptism to believers' baptism, knew life on both sides of the fence. He commented:

> An important sign that a defender of infant baptism is certain that his cause has a sound theological basis ought surely to be . . . that he is able to present and support it calmly. . . . But he cannot become irritated in debating with his opponents. If anyone does become irritated, it is a sign that he feels he has been hit at a vulnerable and unprotected point in his position, that he does not have a good conscience in relation to his cause, that consequently he cannot have a good and quiet conscience in relation to his opponents, and that he has to lay about him all the more violently for this reason.[1]

This, of course, was Barth's warning to his opponents (now paedobaptists) who might take up cudgels against him! The advice surely applies to parties on any side of the question, and it is a testi-

---

[1] Karl Barth, *Church Dogmatics: The Doctrine of Reconciliation* 4/4, ed. G. W. Bromiley and T. F. Torrance, trans. G. W. Bromiley (Edinburgh: T & T Clark, 1969), p. 170.

mony to the "good conscience" and the good arguments of each of the contributors to this book that they commend themselves dispositionally.

If we would rather avoid disagreeable arguments about baptism on the one hand, a good case can be made that we do not take baptism seriously enough. An Asian theologian recently related to me how some Chinese non-Christians view baptism, telling their sons and daughters that it's okay to worship or study the Bible with those Christians, but just don't get baptized! As nonbelievers, they recognize that to be baptized is to cross a river of no return. This perception is strikingly biblical and instructive. Baptism is a serious proposition.

Nothing neutralizes the best theological arguments for the baptism of infants quite like a congregation's impulse to focus on the cute antics of the young babies as they are being baptized. On the other hand, sometimes solemnity is improvised and arrives through the liturgical back door. Perhaps the most arresting baptism I have ever witnessed was in a Baptist church where a young man was being baptized. As the boy came up from the water, his father stood up in the congregation and in a loud voice declared, "This is my beloved son in whom I am well pleased!" He was obviously proud of his son, and he was taking the event with utter seriousness; but I was overcome by the dissonance between this echo of the heavenly voice at Jesus' baptism in the Jordan and this commonplace baptism in the Chicago suburbs.

More recently, I heard a testimony from a middle-aged woman who had been raised in a nonreligious Jewish family but had married a Christian. She had, with her husband, attended an evangelical Presbyterian church for a decade before she was baptized. Her conversion was a very gradual journey. Over the years, when asked if she had considered baptism, she always responded that she would know when she was ready. Finally, she was ready (coinciding, not incidentally, with the planned baptism of her child). Reflecting on her experience of baptism, she commented that she sensed God's love poured out on her in the moment of her baptism. I was struck by the seriousness and thoughtfulness with which she took this step of baptism. Baptism was for her a decisive and demarcating event. Despite its Presbyterian setting, it carried Baptistic overtones. Where the rite touches actual lives, surprises sometimes ensue.

Many, if not most, of the churches in the West operate now in increasingly post-Christian societies. David Wright has argued that our situation is becoming far more like the pre-Constantinian world of the early church.[2] For this reason, in addition to the perennial questions this book explores, the time seems ripe for a thoughtful reconsideration of the meaning of this "one baptism" that we profess as Christians in the midst of increasingly non-Christian Western societies. Alert readers will find this theme surfacing from time to time in this book.

Like so many theological issues, on the surface the practice and meaning of baptism looks like a straightforward question, at least for the Bible-believing evangelical Christian. What does the Scripture say? Well, Scripture says X. Okay then, that settles it.

In actual fact one's view of baptism is bound up with other theological and hermeneutical considerations. As David Wright pointed out in a 1994 essay,[3] the fact of Christian disagreement over baptism raises unsettling questions about the perspicuity, or clarity, of Scripture. As you follow the arguments set out in this book, take note of what each of these advocates counts as persuasive evidence for his view. Is it strictly a matter of what the New Testament teaches? Or is there a larger context—biblical, theological, historical—that comes into play? And what theology of baptism informs the practice that each advocates?

The believers' baptism view, sometimes called credobaptism (credo being Latin for "I believe") view, is represented by Bruce Ware, a

---

[2]David F. Wright, "Recovering Baptism for a New Age of Mission," in *Doing Theology for the People of God: Studies in Honor of J. I. Packer,* ed. Donald Lewis and Alister McGrath (Downers Grove, Ill.: InterVarsity Press, 1996), pp. 51-66.

[3]David F. Wright, "Scripture and Evangelical Diversity with Special Reference to the Baptismal Divide," in *A Pathway into the Holy Scripture,* ed. D. F. Wright and Philip E. Satterthwaite (Grand Rapids: Eerdmans, 1994), pp. 257-75.

Baptist theologian. He argues that only those who have already become believers in Christ should be baptized and that this baptism should be by immersion in water.

The infant baptism view, often called paedobaptism (*paidos* being Greek for "child"), is represented by Sinclair Ferguson, a Presbyterian pastor and theologian. He argues that baptism is the sign and seal of the new covenant work of Christ and is analogous to circumcision, which was the sign of the old covenant of Israel. The biblical continuity between the covenants demands that infants of believers be baptized in addition to those who come to Christ at any age. The mode of baptism is not at issue.

The dual-practice view is argued by Anthony Lane, who in his essay describes something of his personal story of baptismal experience, a biography that has put him on both sides of the issue. His own assessment of the biblical and historical evidence has finally led him to affirm both adult, or convert, baptism and either paedobaptism or adult baptism as legitimate options for those born into a Christian home.

These three views do not represent the full range of Christian views on baptism. For example, Lutheran, Pentecostal, Christian Churches/Churches of Christ, Roman Catholic and Orthodox views are not represented. Even for the three viewpoints that are presented, other advocates of these views would have framed the arguments somewhat differently. But there is a good reason for the three views we have chosen. This book assumes that most of its readers will come from mainstream evangelicalism, and the three views represented make up the most common ones encountered in this broad tradition. Quite obviously, this book assumes that the biggest question on its readers' minds has to do with two significant alternatives: believers' baptism or infant baptism? It is worth noting, too, that our essayists do agree on the fundamental premise that Scripture is the final authority for informing our view of baptism. So each of these contributors is "on the same page" when it comes to appealing to biblical evidence, and this in turn assures a certain level of coherence in the discussion.

Admittedly, we face a hazard in presenting the three views of this book. Readers might judge that, at least so far as they are concerned, the argument arrives at a stalemate between infant and believers' baptism. With a third view available, one that incorporates elements of both of the other views, some readers might naturally gravitate toward the middle road, or "Middle-Lane" (p. 181; cf. p. 188) as Sinclair Ferguson wittily labels it! But this view is not posed as a theological and practical compromise. It is a view that stands foursquare on its own biblical, theological and historical basis. I will leave Bruce Ware and Sinclair Ferguson to bring forth their best arguments against this third option—and Tony Lane to respond in kind.

This is a book that should work well in a variety of classroom settings, particularly in evangelical colleges and seminaries where many of the students come from churches that proclaim and practice one of these three baptismal views. Students will want to know the best arguments for the practice of their own church tradition, but they will also want to know why other Christians—often including their fellow students—practice baptism differently. This book will do a fine job of introducing them to robust arguments for each view. The critiques by fellow essayists will bring out weaknesses and strengths that are not always apparent. In addition to students of theology, inquiring laypeople will also find this book an attractive introduction to the baptismal practice of their own church as well as that of others.

Finally, I need to comment on why I, the InterVarsity Press editor responsible to shepherd this project to publication, am writing this introduction. It is not something I ever planned or aspired to write. On this topic I feel like a Suzuki violin student filling in for Itzhak Perlman. These pages belonged to David Wright, who died before this task was completed. David F. Wright (1937-2008) was born in London and educated at Cambridge in classics and theology. In 1964 he began as a lecturer in the department of ecclesiastical history at New College, University of Edinburgh, and in 1973 was promoted to senior lecturer. In 1999 he was awarded a personal chair in Patristic and Reformed Christianity, reflecting his research, which ranged from the Fathers to the Reformation, including Martin Bucer, John Calvin, John Knox and Peter Martyr Vermigli. He also thought long, researched deeply and wrote much on the topic of baptism.

I think David Wright would have treated us to an introduction that would have been a small classic in itself ("worth the price of the book," as some like to say), and I was looking forward to it. An experienced and exacting editor, Wright completed his work on the essays and responses in this book prior to his death in February 2008 after a protracted bout with prostate cancer. As far as we can determine, he had not found the energy to tackle the introduction.

In the essays that follow, you will find references to David Wright's research and writings on baptism. As a tribute to his work and as a faint outline of the introduction that might have been, it seemed fitting to provide the bibliography (compiled by Anthony Lane) of his work on baptism, which may be found at the back of this book.

In one of his last communications with me (January 14, 2008) he wrote, "I have never yet in all my numerous writings on baptism set myself to consider on a four-square basis how one tackles the disagreements, and the fact of disagreement itself. It should make for a useful introduction, except that I know my mind is no longer working as sharply as it should." I would love to hear his perspective now on "how one tackles the disagreements, and the fact of the disagreement itself"! But perhaps one way to do so is through a thoughtful reading and consideration of this book.

1

BELIEVERS' BAPTISM VIEW

Bruce A. Ware

THE CLOSING WORDS OF THE GOSPEL OF MATTHEW present some of
the most important instructions of the Lord Christ to his redeemed
people: "All authority in heaven and on earth has been given to me.
Go therefore and make disciples of all nations, baptizing them in the
name of the Father and of the Son and of the Holy Spirit, teaching
them to observe all that I have commanded you. And behold, I am
with you always, to the end of the age" (Mt 28:18-20).[1] Despite the
obvious significance of this dominical commissioning, followers of
Christ have entertained both differing understandings and differing
practices, particularly of Christ's command to baptize others. One
would have hoped that Christ's church would uniformly understand
and follow just what Christ instructed. Yet the sad fact is that our
different views of baptism mean that in all likelihood significant
portions of Christ's church are failing to carry out what Christ has
commanded, even if this failure stems from good motives.

In this chapter a case will be made for understanding Christ's
words to mean that those who have *believed* in Jesus Christ should be
immersed in water in obedience to Christ's command.[2] That is,

---

[1]Unless otherwise noted, all Scripture citations are from *The Holy Bible: English Standard
Version* (Wheaton, Ill.: Crossway Bibles, 2001).

[2]For a sustained argument that baptism is only rightly of disciples, see Fred A. Malone,

Christ's imperative here is that only those, but all of those, who have become believers in Christ should be baptized following their conversion to Christ (also referred to as credobaptism) and that their baptism should take place through their immersion in water. The subjects of baptism, then, are believers in Christ and his atoning work. The mode of their baptism is by immersion.

If the argument of this chapter is correct, then it simply is the case that large portions of the church are living in disobedience to Christ, despite the fact that they would deny this is the case and even attempt to defend their own practice of baptizing infants on biblical grounds (also referred to as paedobaptism).[3] While we agree to disagree as brothers and sisters in Christ, our disagreement here must be seen by all followers of Christ as sobering, since we cannot but conclude that obedience to our Lord is at stake in our understanding and practice of the baptism he commanded his followers to practice.

In what follows, I will present a summary of the positive case for believers' baptism by immersion,[4] appealing to biblical, theological and historical support. In the process, reference will be made at various points to other Christian traditions, particularly to the Reformed paedobaptist tradition. While contrasts will be noted with that and other traditions, the main burden of this portion of the chapter is a

---

The Baptism of Disciples Alone: A Covenantal Argument for Credobaptism Versus Paedobaptism (Cape Coral, Fla.: Founders Press, 2003).

[3]Some of the most thorough defenses of paedobaptism are the following: Pierre-Charles Marcel, *The Biblical Doctrine of Infant Baptism: Sacrament of the Covenant of Grace*, trans. Philip Edgcumbe Hughes (London: James Clarke & Co., 1959); Geoffrey W. Bromiley, *Children of Promise: The Case for Baptizing Infants* (Grand Rapids: Eerdmans, 1979); John Murray, *Christian Baptism* (Phillipsburg, N.J.: P & R, 1980); Robert R. Booth, *Children of the Promise: The Biblical Case for Infant Baptism* (Phillipsburg, N.J.: P & R, 1995); Douglas Wilson, *To a Thousand Generations—Infant Baptism: Covenant Mercy for the People of God* (Moscow, Idaho: Canon Press, 1996); and Gregg Strawbridge, ed., *The Case for Covenantal Infant Baptism* (Phillipsburg, N.J.: P & R, 2003).

[4]For fuller treatments, I recommend that the reader consult George R. Beasley-Murray, *Baptism in the New Testament* (Grand Rapids: Eerdmans, 1962); Paul K. Jewett, *Infant Baptism and the Covenant of Grace* (Grand Rapids: Eerdmans, 1978); Malone, *The Baptism of Disciples Alone;* and especially Thomas R. Schreiner and Shawn D. Wright, eds., *Believer's Baptism: Sign of the New Covenant in Christ,* New American Commentary Studies in Bible & Theology 2 (Nashville: B & H, 2007).

presentation of the positive case for the credobaptist position. Following this summary, two brief commendations will be offered for the practical benefits of believers' baptism.

BIBLICAL SUPPORT FOR BELIEVERS' BAPTISM BY IMMERSION

Linguistic argument. First, the term *baptism* refers most clearly and naturally to the immersion of a person in water, and as such, its very usage argues directly for immersion as the mode of baptism, and indirectly for the application of baptism to those past infancy. The root meaning of the word *baptō* is "to dip," "to submerge," "to immerse,"[5] or more explicitly, "to dip in or under."[6] The usages of *baptō* in classical Greek, in the LXX (e.g., 2 Kings 5:14), and in the New Testament all evidence this prevailing meaning. When washing or sprinkling are in view, the more common words used are *louō*, *niptō* or *rhainō*.[7] In the New Testament in particular, *baptō* is used only four times, "and only with the meaning of 'dip.'"[8] *Baptizō* occurs chiefly in the Gospels for John's baptism, in the form of immersion, and in the rest of the New Testament for Christian baptism. Oepke notes that the intensified form, *baptizō*, is used in the sense of "immerse" from the time of Hippocrates forward in such contexts, for example, of the sinking of a ship in water or of one who drowns in water.[9] Clearly the biblical terms for "baptism" have the prevailing meaning associated with immersion.[10]

Contextual argument. The contextual usage of these terms in the

---

[5]G. R. Beasley-Murray, "Baptism," *NIDNTT* 1:144.

[6]Albrecht Oepke, "*baptō, baptizō*," *TDNT* 1:529.

[7]G. R. Beasley-Murray, "Baptism," *NIDNTT* 1:144.

[8]Ibid., 1:145.

[9]Oepke, "*baptō, baptizō*," 1:530.

[10]One cannot help but wonder how the church's grappling with the issue of baptism might have been altered had the translators of our earliest English Bibles actually translated *baptō* and *baptizō* instead of transliterating the term. If we had read in our English Bibles that Jesus was "immersed" in the Jordan by John the Baptist, or that Jesus commanded his followers to make disciples, "immersing" them in the name of the Father, and of the Son, and of the Holy Spirit—one cannot help wonder how differently the thinking of Christian people may have been.

New Testament supports this simple linguistic argument. For example, following Jesus' baptism by John the Baptist, we see Jesus described as coming "up from the water" (Mt 3:16) or "up out of the water" (Mk 1:10). It is noteworthy that a very careful Roman Catholic scholar, John Meier, argues that John the Baptist practiced immersion.

> That John's baptism involved immersion of the candidates' body is implied by the statement that, after Jesus' baptism, he "came up out of the water" (Mark 1:10 || Matt 3:16). This supposition is bolstered (1) by the Baptist's focus on the Jordan River and on Aenon-near-Salim, in which he baptized "because there was an abundance of water there" (John 3:23); and (2) by Josephus' statements in the *Antiquities* that John baptized not to cleanse souls but to purify bodies.[11]

Similarly in the account of Philip baptizing the eunuch from Ethiopia, we read that Philip and the eunuch "both went down into the water" (Acts 8:38), and then both "came up out of the water" (Acts 8:39). Similar accounts can be found in some early church documents closest in time to the New Testament period itself. *The Shepherd* of Hermas (ca. A.D. 140-155), for example, speaks of some who believed the preaching of the gospel as having descended "into the water, and again ascended."[12] Stander and Louw comment, "Obviously the phrases 'going down' and 'coming up' are used to focus on the two processes involved in immersion."[13] Clearly the evidence from such accounts favors strongly the notion that baptism was by immersion.

---

[11]John P. Meier, *A Marginal Jew: Rethinking the Historical Jesus*, vol. 2, *Mentor, Message, and Miracles* (New York: Doubleday, 1994), p. 93 n. 152.

[12]Hermas *Shepherd*, Similitude 9.16; as quoted in Hendrick Stander and Johannes Louw, *Baptism in the Early Church*, rev. ed. (Webster, N.Y.: Cary Publications, 2005), p. 20. Note: my thanks are extended to Professor Michael Haykin for making me aware of this very helpful historical resource.

[13] Stander and Louw, *Baptism in the Early Church*, p. 20. Stander and Louw, *Baptism in the Early Church*, p. 25, argue similarly for understanding the prevailing practice of the early church to be that of immersion from several other citations of various church fathers and documents, included among them Aristides of Athens, Clement of Alexandria (p. 31), Tertullian (pp. 36-37), Hippolytus (p. 42) and Basil the Great (who practiced tri-immersion, p. 82).

All of the evidence taken together makes a compelling case for understanding the mode of baptism in the New Testament as done by immersion. While this argument relates directly to the question of mode of baptism, it also favors indirectly the idea that the subjects of baptism were not infants.[14] We simply do not see either in the New Testament or in the early church any clear practice of immersing infants.[15] If it can be sustained that the mode of baptism in the New Testament is immersion, this clearly, then, lends support to the idea that those so immersed were well beyond their infancy. Even if "children" are baptized in the New Testament and in the early church, we certainly must distinguish "children" generally from "infants" specifically. The notion that infants were baptized by immersion simply has no support. That baptism was by immersion, then, fits best, to say the least, with the idea of the subjects of baptism being at least young children and older, while it certainly does not relate to infants.

Instruction and practice of baptism in the New Testament. Every New Testament instruction or command regarding baptism, and every clear instance of baptism that we see in the New Testament, relates to the baptism of those who have repented of sin (John's baptism) and come to faith in Christ (baptisms from Pentecost forward). In other words the strongest support from New Testament evidence favors the position of believers' baptism. Clearly the baptism of John the Baptist was a baptism for those who had repented of sin in anticipation of the Messiah's coming (Mk 1:4-8). Such baptism, with the subjects confessing their sin and responding to John's call for repentance (Mk 1:4-5), sim-

---

[14]I am aware that this argument would have less force for members of Greek Orthodox churches, which often practice infant immersion. Nonetheless the practice of infant immersion performed in Greek Orthodoxy still was not practiced either in the NT or in the early church.

[15]Stander and Louw, *Baptism in the Early Church*, pp. 29-33, comment that some early church texts might be interpreted as indicating the immersion of infants, but these interpretations can be shown to be far less likely than some others—for example, that the immersion was of "children" who were not infants per se or of those who were "children" in the faith. See, for example, their discussion of the baptism by immersion of "children" in Clement of Alexandria.

ply cannot align with infant baptism. These subjects of baptism, rather, are fully aware of the state of their souls and hence follow John's command to prepare for the Messiah's coming (Mk 1:8).

The Matthean Great Commission text, likewise, commands followers of Christ to "make disciples" (aorist imperative, *mathēteusate*) through the dual means of "baptizing" them and "teaching" them (both present participles) all that Christ has commanded them. This, likewise, seems to indicate that those baptized are also able to be taught—hence, they are at least young children or adults, but not infants. Concerning the question of the subjects who are in view here as being baptized, Andreas Köstenberger comments:

> Jesus' command to his followers to make disciples of all nations and to baptize and teach them clearly presupposes that the recipients of baptism and teaching are of sufficient age and maturity that they can consciously choose to be baptized and be instructed in the principles of the Christian faith. Even advocates of infant baptism such as Daniel Doriani acknowledge that "[d]oubtless, the conversion of adults is on Jesus' mind in Matthew 28:18-20."[16]

Despite his admission that adults were on Jesus' mind, Doriani suggests further that "combined with the faith of an adult convert, or with the faith of parents in the case of an infant, baptism both signifies and mediates a relationship with Jesus."[17] In fact, says Doriani, nothing in the Matthean text excludes infants, and certainly even "God in his grace can regenerate a child from the earliest age, even in conjunction with baptism itself." He continues, "wise parents tell their children about their [infant] baptism."[18]

Köstenberger takes note of these claims and provides some apt

---

[16]Andreas J. Köstenberger, "Baptism in the Gospels," in *Believer's Baptism: Sign of the New Covenant in Christ,* ed. Thomas R. Schreiner and Shawn D. Wright, New American Commentary Studies in Bible & Theology 2 (Nashville: B & H, 2007), p. 24. Köstenberger's reference is to Daniel M. Doriani, "Matthew 28:18-20 and the Institution of Baptism," in *The Case for Covenantal Infant Baptism,* ed. Gregg Strawbridge (Phillipsburg, N.J.: P & R, 2003), p. 41.
[17]Doriani, "Matthew 28:18-20," p. 42.
[18]Ibid.

responses. First, Doriani's claim that baptism mediates a relationship with Jesus combined with the faith of parents simply has no basis in the text. Rather these are converts who have responded personally, are baptized, and are taught. Second, the suggestion that God can regenerate "a child from the earliest age" is very problematic, since it seems to imply baptismal regeneration. Third, the suggestion that baptism is a means of teaching children is not what Jesus says. Rather those who are baptized are then taught all that Jesus commanded; Jesus is not suggesting that they later be taught about their infant baptism. Last, to Doriani's claim that nothing in this text excludes infants, Köstenberger replies that nothing in Matthew suggests that infants ought to be baptized. While children may be capable of coming to faith and being taught the commands of Christ, this is not true of infants; hence Jesus' words here do not apply to infants.[19]

Beyond what we learn from John's baptism and Jesus' Great Commission, we find that the rest of the New Testament so links water baptism with newness of life and the reception of the Spirit, that the most compelling understanding of the subjects of baptism identifies them as believers. The book of Acts alone presents several clear instances of believers' baptism, and often links their water baptism to their newness of life in Christ and to their reception of the Spirit. The following list includes these texts from Acts, noting (by the use of italics) the relation in each text between prior belief and subsequent baptism:

> Acts 2:38-39: Peter said to them, "*Repent* and be *baptized* every one of you in the name of Jesus Christ for the forgiveness of your sins, and you will receive the gift of the Holy Spirit. For the promise is for you and for your children and for all who are far off, everyone whom the Lord our God calls to himself."

> Acts 2:41: So those who *received his word* were *baptized*, and there were added that day about three thousand souls.

---

[19]Andreas J. Köstenberger, "Baptism in the Gospels," pp. 24-26.

Acts 8:12-13: But when they *believed* Philip as he preached good news about the kingdom of God and the name of Jesus Christ, they were *baptized*, both men and women. Even Simon himself *believed*, and after being *baptized* he continued with Philip. And seeing signs and great miracles performed, he was amazed.

Acts 8:35-38: Then Philip opened his mouth, and beginning with this Scripture he told him the *good news about Jesus*. And as they were going along the road they came to some water, and the eunuch said, "See, here is water! What prevents me from being *baptized?*" And he commanded the chariot to stop, and they both went down into the water, Philip and the eunuch, and he baptized him.

Acts 9:18: And immediately something like *scales fell from his eyes*, and he regained his sight. Then he rose and was *baptized*.

Acts 10:47-48: "Can anyone withhold water for *baptizing* these people, *who have received the Holy Spirit* just as we have?" And he commanded them to be baptized in the name of Jesus Christ. Then they asked him to remain for some days.

Acts 16:14-15: One who heard us was a woman named Lydia, from the city of Thyatira, a seller of purple goods, who was a worshiper of God. The *Lord opened her heart* to pay attention to what was said by Paul. And after she was *baptized*, and her household as well, she urged us, saying, "If you have judged me to be faithful to the Lord, come to my house and stay." And she prevailed upon us.

Acts 16:32-34: And they *spoke the word of the Lord* to him and to all who were in his house. And he took them the same hour of the night and washed their wounds; and he was *baptized* at once, he and all his family. Then he brought them up into his house and set food before them. And he rejoiced along with his entire household that *he had believed in God*.

Acts 18:8: Crispus, the ruler of the synagogue, *believed* in the Lord, together with his entire household. And many of the Corinthians hearing Paul *believed* and were *baptized*.

Acts 19:3-5: And he said, "Into what then were you baptized?" They said, "Into John's baptism." And Paul said, "John baptized with the baptism of repentance, telling the people to believe in the one who was to come after him, that is, *Jesus.*" *On hearing this,* they were *baptized* in the name of the Lord Jesus.

Acts 22:16: And now why do you wait? Rise and be *baptized* and *wash away your sins,* calling on his name.

While some would want to appeal to the "household" baptisms among these passages from Acts as evidence of infant baptism, I will argue below that these texts provide no compelling evidence for such a view. Rather what these texts testify to over and over again is that baptism follows the reception of the gospel and faith in Christ. Examples of believers' baptism, then, are explicit and plentiful, establishing the New Testament pattern that saving faith precedes and grounds Christian baptism.

Consider also Paul's references to baptism in both Romans 6:3-4 and Colossians 2:12. In both cases the appeal to baptism intends to signify precisely these believers' death to their old life and their regeneration and conversion to newness of life. The sign of baptism is a sign of new life, the very symbolism of a believer's baptism by immersion. Their being dipped under the water signifies their death in Christ, and their being lifted out of the water signifies their newness of life in Christ. Only baptism by immersion provides the symbolism of dying to the old and being raised to new life in Christ.[20]

Unless one holds that baptized infants are regenerated and become recipients of the Spirit and new life in Christ, their infant baptism fails in its function as a sign of an objectively true spiritual reality. Indeed Paul rules out infant baptism in Colossians 2:12, for he says that this new life becomes a reality "through faith." Faith is not possible for infants. Faith is based on understanding, since Paul says that "faith comes from hearing, and hearing through the word of Christ" (Rom 10:17). For baptism to function truly as a sign of

---

[20]Thomas R. Schreiner, "Baptism in the Epistles: An Initiation Rite for Believers," in *Believer's Baptism: Sign of the New Covenant in Christ,* ed. Thomas R. Schreiner and Shawn D. Wright, New American Commentary Studies in Bible & Theology 2 (Nashville: B & H, 2007), pp. 74-79.

regeneration, conversion and new life by the Spirit, the one baptized must have experienced inwardly the spiritual reality which baptism so beautifully portrays. Schreiner comments:

> We have, then, compelling grounds to reject infant baptism. We have seen consistently that those who are baptized have been regenerated by or received the Spirit (Tit 3:5; 1 Cor 12:13). It is difficult to see how the reception of the Spirit could be predicated of infants since the Spirit is received by faith (Gal 3:2, 5) and infants do not exercise faith. Moreover, the Spirit leads believers to a transformed life, so that they bear the fruit of the Spirit instead of the works of the flesh (Gal 5:16-26; cp. Rom 8:1-17) and it is not easy to see how one can speak of infants being transformed by the Spirit. In Rom 6:1-14 and Col 2:11-15 those who are baptized are said to be dead to sin and alive to God in Christ Jesus.[21]

A clear reading of these Pauline texts shows the unmistakable link between water baptism and Spirit baptism, or between the baptism of a believer in water and the spiritual reality of conversion and transformation that has occurred in the believer's life. Only if one wishes to defend baptismal regeneration can one rightly associate infant baptism with these spiritual realities. The most natural and clearest reading of these texts supports the position that the subjects of baptism are believers. The sign of baptism corresponds to the reality of spiritual conversion that has already taken place in their lives.

What is true for Paul is also true for Peter. First Peter 3:21 makes especially clear that baptism is linked with the faith of the one baptized. It reads, "Baptism, which corresponds to this, now saves you, not as a removal of dirt from the body but as an appeal to God for a good conscience, through the resurrection of Jesus Christ." While baptism in itself, seen merely as an act which cleanses the outside of the body, does not save in and of itself, baptism which expresses an appeal to God for forgiveness through the death and resurrection of Christ is salvific. The NIV reads, "pledge of a good conscience to-

---

[21]Schreiner, "Baptism in the Epistles," p. 93.

ward God" in place of the ESV's "appeal to God for a good conscience." Most commentators favor "appeal" over "pledge."[22] In either case the one being baptized is taking some action toward God. Such action rules out infant baptism. As Schreiner comments:

> what is said here does not fit with infant baptism, for infants cannot appeal to God for a good conscience or pledge to maintain a good conscience before God. Peter exalts the work of Christ in saving his people, but that work produces an effect in the consciousness and life of the believer. The teaching of 1 Peter on baptism, then, fits with the notion that baptism was not applied to infants.[23]

Both Peter and Paul see baptism as a sign of the renewal of life that comes through faith in Christ. For the sign (baptism) to be administered, the reality (new life in Christ by faith) must have first taken place. Belief, in short, precedes and grounds the legitimacy of baptism.

Absence of nonbelievers' baptism in the New Testament. Not only does every New Testament instruction or command regarding baptism and every clear instance of baptism that we see in the New Testament relate to the baptism of believers, the New Testament also offers no clear and unmistakable instance of nonbelievers' or infant baptism. These two points together are important to grasp. If all of the New Testament evidence shows baptism as being connected with those who exercise faith, and no instance can be shown otherwise, it would seem that an extraordinary burden of proof would lie at the feet of those who would propose that infant baptism is, nonetheless, biblical and supportable.

Of course many have proposed seeing infant baptism indicated in various places in the New Testament, and so we must consider these and evaluate whether infants in fact are in view. Some cite the household baptism of the Philippian jailer (Acts 16:33), for example, as a likely example of infant baptism. On learning that Paul and Silas had

---

[22]See the extended discussion by Thomas R. Schreiner, *1, 2 Peter, Jude*, New American Commentary (Nashville: Broadman & Holman, 2003), 37:193-97.

[23]Schreiner, "Baptism in the Epistles," p. 71.

not fled the jail when they had opportunity, the jailer, filled with
fear, fell down before them and said, "Sirs, what must I do to be
saved?" (Acts 16:30). The account continues:

> And they said, "Believe in the Lord Jesus, and you will be saved, you
> and your household." And they spoke the word of the Lord to him
> and to all who were in his house. And he took them the same hour
> of the night and washed their wounds; and he was baptized at once,
> he and all his family. Then he brought them up into his house and set
> food before them. And he rejoiced along with his entire household
> that he had believed in God. (Acts 16:31-34)

Concerning this text and its relevance to infant baptism, Bryan
Chapell comments:

> The account of the baptism of the Philippian jailer's household is
> particularly instructive because of the precise description supplied
> by Luke, the writer of Acts. Luke says that *all* of the jailer's house-
> hold was baptized (Acts 16:33), but then he uses a *singular* verb to
> describe who rejoiced and believed in God that night (Acts 16:34).
> The jailer himself believed (singular verb), and his whole house was
> baptized. Sadly this important distinction in the account is not re-
> flected is some of our modern translations (see the English Standard
> Version for an excellent translation). As a result, some assume that
> the entire households were baptized in the New Testament because
> everyone in them believed the gospel. While this is not impossible,
> it is unlikely that all those households consisted only of those who
> were old enough to make an intelligent faith commitment. Further,
> the assumption that everyone in those households must have made a
> faith commitment does not take notice of the careful distinction that
> Luke makes between those who actually believed and those who
> were baptized.[24]

Since this is the strongest of the "household" accounts appealed to
by advocates of infant baptism, it should be examined closely. Chapell
is correct to observe the use of the singular verbs in Acts 16:34, i.e.,

[24]Bryan Chapell, "A Pastoral View of Infant Baptism," in *The Case for Covenantal Infant
Baptism,* ed. Gregg Strawbridge (Phillipsburg, N.J.: P & R, 2003), pp. 20-21.

it was the jailer who is said to have "rejoiced" (3rd singular, aorist, middle, indicative of *agalliaō*) and "believed" (perfect, active, participle, masculine, nominative, singular of *pisteuō*) in God. And, yes, his whole household was baptized (Acts 16:33). However, Chapell omits several other pertinent observations about this text, ones that clearly lead to a very different conclusion than what Chapell has suggested.

First, Paul and Silas are said to have spoken the word of the Lord both to the jailer himself and also "to all who were in his house" (Acts 16:32). Since Luke mentions here that the word was spoken to *all* in the house, one might assume from this that all were able to understand the speaking of that word. In other words this detail would suggest that if there were children in the jailer's house (which we are never told explicitly, but it is reasonable to assume), they were likely not infants. Since all heard the word spoken, the most likely inference is that all were capable of understanding what was spoken.

Second, Acts 16:33 states the baptism of the jailer also by use of a singular ("and he was baptized at once," where "baptized" is third singular, aorist, passive, indicative of *baptizō*). Luke follows this statement with an elaboration indicating that not just the jailer alone was baptized, for he was baptized, "he and all his family." This picks up on Luke's focus on the jailer himself. Luke's account likely flows out of the fact that the jailer asked the question, "Sirs, what must I do to be saved?" (Acts 16:30). Luke's entire discussion of this account puts stress on the jailer, while adding that his family is included in this offer of salvation. Both Acts 16:32 and Acts 16:33 show this pattern of focusing on the jailer but then including the household as well.

Third, Acts 16:34 continues the same pattern of description; the focus remains directly on the jailer and his actions, but those in his house are also involved. In light of this, Chapell's account of this verse is somewhat misleading since his description of this verse omits Luke's inclusion of the mention of the jailer's household. The reader will recall that Chapell had said, "The jailer himself believed (singular verb) [Acts 16:34], and his whole house was baptized [Acts

16:33]," Luke making a careful distinction "between those who actually believed and those who were baptized." But the grammar of our text suggests something different from what Chapell indicates. As we have seen, in Acts 16:33 the jailer is said to be baptized (singular), followed by the elaboration, "he and all his family," indicating that both he and the members of his household were baptized. In Acts 16:34 (NASB), something of the same pattern is evident. Here the jailer "rejoiced . . . having believed in God," to be sure.

The verse also includes a phrase (in Greek, it is a single term, *panoikei*) between the singular verbs "he rejoiced" and "he had believed." The ESV renders the Greek term "with his entire household." Yes, Luke states explicitly that the jailer rejoiced, having believed in God. Luke also includes another word that indicates that the jailer did so along with all of those in his house. Whether the phrase "with his entire household" goes with "rejoiced" or "believed" is difficult to say. F. F. Bruce comments, "Here the adverb [*panoikei*, "with his entire household"] may be taken grammatically with either *ēgalliasato* ["he rejoiced"] or *pepisteukōs* ["he having believed"]; in sense it probably goes with both."[25] If the "household" phrase goes only with the rejoicing, this would exclude infants who would be incapable of comprehending what had occurred in order to rejoice. Or if the "household" phrase goes with believing, clearly this would indicate that all in the house were of an age to understand and believe the gospel. If Bruce is correct and the "household" phrase goes with both the rejoicing and the believing, we have strong reason to dismiss the notion that the jailer's household included infants.

What makes the most sense here is that in Acts 16:34 the same pattern of focusing on the jailer while including his household continues. The offer of salvation is given to the jailer specifically while including also his house (Acts 16:31). Paul and Silas spoke the word of the Lord specifically to the jailer, but included with him were all

---

[25]F. F. Bruce, *The Acts of the Apostles*, 3rd rev. ed. (Grand Rapids: Eerdmans, 1990), p. 365.

who were in his house (Acts 16:32). Then the jailer was baptized (singular verb), he along with all of his family (Acts 16:33). Finally, he rejoiced and believed in God, along with his entire household (Acts 16:34).

What seems clear, then, is that while Luke focuses attention on the jailer who asked initially how he could be saved, he includes in each succeeding step both the jailer himself (as the focus) and all of his house. Included in this, then, is the notion that as the jailer believed and rejoiced, so did his whole family with him believe in God and rejoice. Commenting on the use of this text by paedobaptists, Robert Stein aptly states, "It is highly selective, on the one hand, to include infants in the baptism of the 'entire family' of the jailor and then, on the other hand, to exclude them from the 'entire family' that believes and rejoices in their new faith (Acts 16:34). This would be a clear case of special pleading."[26] So it would seem.

Fourth and finally, even though it has been shown that Chapell's interpretation—that the jailer alone believed yet all in his household were baptized—should be rejected, it is worth pointing out one interesting and somewhat troubling implication of Chapell's view, should it be taken seriously and applied. Unless Chapell is prepared to say that the jailer was the only person older than infancy in his family, that is, that all the members of his family were infants and only infants, then one ends up with a very odd situation. Let's say, for example, that the jailer's household included his wife and a teenager or two. If the jailer alone believed, yet all in his household were baptized, this would mean that his unbelieving wife and unbelieving older children were baptized on his (and his alone) belief and salvation. I wonder if Chapell would recommend this practice in paedobaptist churches today.

When the father of an unsaved home comes to faith in Christ, would it be pastorally correct to urge on him the baptism of all who

---

[26]Robert H. Stein, "Baptism in Luke-Acts," in *Believer's Baptism: Sign of the New Covenant in Christ*, ed. Thomas R. Schreiner and Shawn D. Wright, New American Commentary Studies in Bible & Theology 2 (Nashville: B & H, 2007), p. 63.

are in his house, including his wife and adult children still at home? What this shows is further reason for thinking that Chapell has simply missed the obvious meaning of this text, all in order somehow to see infants as part of the jailer's household, which, recall, the text never says. The most likely reading of this account is that as the jailer heard and believed the gospel, so too his whole family heard and believed the gospel. As a result, he and his entire household of believers were baptized. Assuming that the jailer's household included infants simply does not work in this text.

None of the other "household" passages in the New Testament fares better for infant baptism than Acts 16:25-34. Though they mention along with a convert his or her household—for example, Cornelius and his household (Acts 10:48), Lydia and her household (Acts 16:15), Crispus and his household (Acts 18:8), the household of Stephanas (1 Cor 1:16)—there never is specific mention that infants were among those in the household who were baptized. To assume that there were is simply to add to what the text says. Further, some texts indicate the same kind of "household" faith as we saw in Acts 16:32-34 (e.g., "Crispus . . . believed . . . together with his entire household"—Acts 18:8). In any case, having seen in Acts 16 how implausible it is that infants were among the jailer's household, and this in the one text that affords us the most detail and explanation, it simply cannot be sustained from the New Testament that these household texts rightly support infant baptism.

Can infant baptism be seen or rightly inferred from elsewhere in the New Testament? In Strawbridge's *Case for Covenantal Infant Baptism*, two passages (not yet mentioned) in particular received regular attention from various contributors, and the Scripture index confirms the regularity with which these are referenced. These seemingly "favorite" texts for supporting infant baptism are Acts 2:38-39 and 1 Corinthians 7:14. In light of the strength with which appeal is made to these, some comment is required.

First, regarding Acts 2:38-39, Joel Beeke and Ray Lanning assert that the promise Peter mentions is "rhetorical shorthand for the covenant of grace, which embodies the promise of salvation that he calls upon his hearers to embrace."[27] Further, they note that when Peter says, "unto you, and to your children," Peter "included children in Acts 2:39 on account of the content and structure of God's covenant fellowship with his people ever since the days of Abraham."[28] The relevance of this understanding for infant baptism is significant. They explain:

> We have to remind ourselves that the multitude who heard Peter's sermon on Pentecost was Jewish. It included Jews from Palestine, proselytes, and dispersed Jews from other parts of the Roman Empire and beyond. The Old Testament was all they had of the Holy Scriptures. As they listened to Peter preaching from those Scriptures (twelve of the twenty-two verses of Peter's sermon in Acts 2 contain quotations from the Old Testament), they could have understood his words in only one way—as a reference to the promise in God's covenant and the fact that that promise extended not only to believers but to their children as well. To interpret Acts 2:39 in light of the New Testament Scriptures, which did not yet exist, as do many Baptists, is to engage in hermeneutical error and can only lead to a serious misrepresentation of the mind of the Spirit.[29]

Some responses are needed. First, it seems doubtful that the "promise" to which Peter refers in Acts 2:39 ("For the promise is for you") is meant to take his hearers back to the Abrahamic covenant per se. No doubt all that is happening at this time, with the coming of the Messiah and the pouring out of the Spirit, all relates directly to the fulfillment of God's original promise to Abraham that through him (i.e., through his seed, Messiah) all the nations would be blessed. Indeed this certainly is in the background (evidence for this seems to come from Is 44:3 and Gal 3:14). But the "promise" of Acts 2:39 is more specific or more narrow than this. Surely in Acts 2:39 Peter is

---

[27]Joel R. Beeke and Ray B. Lanning, "Unto You, and to Your Children," in *The Case for Covenantal Infant Baptism,* ed. Gregg Strawbridge (Phillipsburg, N.J.: P & R, 2003), p. 55.

[28]Ibid.

[29]Ibid., pp. 56-57.

simply referring to the very promise that he has just stated in Acts 2:38. That is, he had said to those listening, "Repent and be baptized every one of you in the name of Jesus Christ for the forgiveness of your sins, and you will receive the gift of the Holy Spirit" (Acts 2:38). Does it not stand to reason that when Peter continues, "For the promise is for you," he has in mind the promise he has just given his listeners in his preceding statement? In other words, Peter wants his listeners to know that the promise of the long-awaited indwelling Holy Spirit (cf. Is 32:15-20; 44:1-5; Ezek 36:26-32; and, of course, Joel 2:28-32, quoted by Peter in Acts 2:16-21), who had just been poured out at Pentecost, could also be theirs if they would but repent and be baptized.

The promise then is the promise specifically of the outpouring of the Holy Spirit of which Peter just spoke, not merely and more generally a continuation of the promise of the Abrahamic covenant per se. This is supported further by Jesus' statement to the anxious disciples in Acts 1:4-5: "[Jesus] ordered them not to depart from Jerusalem, but to wait for the *promise* of the Father, which, he said, 'you heard from me; for John baptized with water, but you will be baptized with the Holy Spirit not many days from now'" (italics added). So surely the promise that Peter conveys in Acts 2:39 is the very promise Jesus had given to them, that is, of the indwelling Holy Spirit who would come upon those who trust in Christ.

Second, Peter states that this promise is "for you and for your children *and for all who are far off*, everyone whom the Lord our God calls to himself" (Acts 2:39, italics added). The fact that Peter does not stop with merely saying, "the promise is for you and for your children," but adds also, "and for all who are far off," shows that he does not have in mind some supposed continuation of the sign of the Abrahamic covenant in which the children of believers are the recipients of the sign of the covenant (now, infant baptism in place of circumcision).

The promise extends far beyond the children of believers, to all who are far off. So either the covenant of grace, now signified through the sign of baptism, should be applied to the children of believers *and to all people everywhere*, or it is the case that this simply is not what Peter means. Clearly what Peter means here is that the promise of receiving the indwelling Holy Spirit through repentance and faith in Christ is a promise that is just as much for your own children (as they repent of their sin and trust Christ) and for all people everywhere (as they repent of their sin and trust in Christ) as it is for you, that is, those listening to Peter preaching on the day of Pentecost. This does not suggest then that we should baptize our infants but rather that we should share the gospel with them, as we should with all who are far off (cf. Acts 1:8), so that they learn and know that they too can receive this promised gift through repentance and faith.

Third, the last phrase of Acts 2:39, "everyone whom the Lord our God calls to himself," also argues against the use of this verse to support infant baptism. The fulfillment of this promise will occur, says Peter, in all of those—all of those children of the hearers, and all of those who are far off whom God will call to himself. In other words, God will not fail to give this promised Holy Spirit to all of those whom he has elected and so will call efficaciously to himself. Hence, while the offer of this promise can rightly go to all people, including all children of believers, the fulfillment of the promise will be in the lives only of those whom God calls to himself. Not all of the children, necessarily, nor all of those who are far off, necessarily, will actually receive what is offered them in the promise. But be assured: all of those children, and all of those far off, whom God calls—*all* of them will receive this promised gift. Given these three observations about this text, it seems abundantly clear that Peter's reference to children here has no relation whatsoever to some supposed practice of infant baptism as the continuation of the sign of the covenant to Abraham.

Another text cited often in support of infant baptism is 1 Corinthians 7:14. This verse reads, "For the unbelieving husband is made holy because of his wife, and the unbelieving wife is made holy be-

cause of her husband. Otherwise your children would be unclean,
but as it is, they are holy." Commenting on this text, Bryan Chapell
says:

> Few verses in Scripture more forcefully indicate that God communi-
> cates his grace to children while they are in the household of a cov-
> enant parent. Scripture does not contend that an adult who has
> turned from his parent's faith can presume to receive the eternal sal-
> vation promised through Abraham's covenant, but, while children
> remain under the authority of a believing parent, they are repre-
> sented covenantally by that parent's faith.[30]

Also relating 1 Corinthians 7:14 to infant baptism, Richard Pratt
suggests,

> Interestingly enough, in 1 Corinthians 7:14 this concept of sancti-
> fication is applied, not only to unbelieving spouses, but also to the
> children of such marriages. . . . Until Christ returns in glory, it is
> not only permissible and helpful, but also necessary, to speak of
> certain people as consecrated or sanctified to God by their close
> associations with the people of God and with the activities of true
> believers. For this reason, it is quite appropriate to speak of the
> children of believers as sanctified or consecrated by their involve-
> ment in the more external aspects of life in the new covenant, even
> though they may not be regenerated. So the internalization prom-
> ised in the new covenant by no means proscribes the baptism of
> infants.[31]

The paedobaptist argument here is rather indirect and complex:
since children are considered holy by virtue of living in the home
of a believing parent, they are considered participants within the
new covenant, though they may not yet be regenerate. As such
they should rightly participate in the sign of the covenant, baptism,
and so their infant baptism should be seen as legitimate, as it is applied to these unregenerate participants of the new covenant. In

---

[30]Chapell, "A Pastoral View of Infant Baptism," p. 13.
[31]Richard L. Pratt Jr., "Infant Baptism in the New Covenant," in *The Case for Covenantal Infant Baptism,* ed. Gregg Strawbridge (Phillipsburg, N.J.: P & R, 2003), p. 172.

responding to the use of this text in support of infant baptism, it should be observed first that the text says nothing about baptism, infant or otherwise. A huge theological leap is being made here from the stated "holiness" of these children to implying their place in the new covenant and then further implying the legitimacy of their infant baptism. So much is assumed in this argument that can be challenged. As the text stands, there simply is no direct statement about baptism.

Second, Paul speaks of the unbelieving spouse in the same way as he does of the children living in the home of this believer. That is, both the unbelieving spouse and the children in this home are considered "holy" by virtue of their being in a home with one believing spouse/parent. If the stated holiness of the children indicates their place in the new covenant, would not paedobaptists have to say that the same is true of the unbelieving spouse? If not, why not? But if so, would not the sign of the covenant—baptism—rightly be administered to this adult as well? Whatever is concluded about the holiness of the children should in turn be concluded about the holiness of the unbelieving spouse.

Third, is it not likely that Paul's point is much simpler and more straightforward than the complicated argument made by paedobaptists? Paul is admonishing the believing spouse in a marriage not to leave or divorce when his or her spouse is an unbeliever (1 Cor 7:12-13). To support this admonition, he then states in 1 Corinthians 7:14 that the unbelieving spouse is "made holy" by the ongoing presence in the home of the believer.

Clearly, Paul is not saying that this unbelieving spouse is saved because he or she is married to a believer (cf. 1 Cor 7:16). Nor is he saying that the unbelieving spouse is part of the new covenant. Rather he is simply saying that the presence of the believer in the home causes any unbeliever in the home, whether a spouse or children, to be "set apart" to gospel witness and to the possibility of salvation due to that witness, which would come to an end if the believing spouse were to leave.

He continues in 1 Corinthians 7:15 to say that if the unbelieving spouse leaves anyway, despite the attempts made by the believing spouse to bear witness to the gospel, then there is no more that can be done. But the believer should stay, if the unbeliever is willing to live in this "mixed" relationship, for who knows whether the unbelieving spouse might be saved (1 Cor 7:16). The children in this context are simply added because they too are "set apart" to this same gospel witness by the ongoing presence of the believing parent in the home. It is a far stretch from this simple understanding to the more elaborate view of covenant participation and legitimacy of infant baptism, none of which is either implied by the text or needed to understand Paul's meaning in this text.

We have, then, no clear examples in the New Testament of the practice of infant baptism, while instead we have observed that all instances of New Testament baptism are of believers. It is no wonder, then, that David Wright wrote in 1987 that "among New Testament scholars the view is increasingly widespread that infant baptism was not practiced in the New Testament Churches,"[32] and more recently that "an emerging majority view among New Testament scholars" is "that infant baptism cannot be confidently claimed to be apostolic. . . . The core conviction of Baptist theology, that the New Testament attests faith-baptism as the norm, is now more widely accepted than at any time since the fourth century, i.e., prior to Augustine."[33] Indeed the case for believers' baptism stands uncontested when one examines all of the relevant evidence from the New Testament.

---

[32]David F. Wright, "The Origins of Infant Baptism—Child Believer's Baptism?" *Scottish Journal of Theology* 40 (1987): 3.

[33]David F. Wright, Book Review of Gregg Strawbridge, ed., *The Case for Covenantal Infant Baptism* (Phillipsburg, N.J.: P & R, 2003), in *Themelios* 30, no. 3 (2005): 118. Wright's main reason for introducing this observation is to register his own criticism of the Strawbridge volume, that in making its case for covenantal infant baptism, the volume as a whole showed little and only partial awareness of this newly emerged consensus among New Testament scholarship that favors Baptist theology.

THEOLOGY OF BAPTISM AS THE SIGN OF THE NEW COVENANT

One area where most credobaptists and most paedobaptists agree is this: baptism is the sign and seal of the new covenant, inaugurated by Christ's death and resurrection, signifying the promise for the one baptized that sins are forgiven, that new life in Christ is received, and that God gives the person a new heart and the indwelling Holy Spirit, by faith.[34]

Where they differ, however, is over the question of the relation of this new covenant sign of baptism to the sign of circumcision, extending from the promise to Abraham (Gen 17:1-14) and continued in the old covenant. Does baptism rightly function today as paedobaptists claim, that is, as performed on infants in anticipation of a future day of belief in Christ and reception of all the blessings attending this faith, in a manner parallel to how circumcision was intended to function under the old covenant? In brief the credobaptist position is that baptism, the sign of the new covenant, should only rightly be administered to believers in Christ Jesus, because by its very nature the new covenant incorporates exclusively those who have turned from their sin through faith in Christ's atoning work on their behalf.[35] In other words, while there is much significant conti-

---

[34]The paedobaptist J. I. Packer, for example, provides a definition of baptism that any Baptist would relish. He writes, "Christian baptism . . . is a sign from God that signifies inward cleansing and remission of sins (Acts 22:16; 1 Cor 6:11; Eph 5:25-27), Spirit-wrought regeneration and new life (Titus 3:5), and the abiding presence of the Holy Spirit as God's seal testifying and guaranteeing that one will be kept safe in Christ forever (1 Cor 12:13; Eph 1:13-14). Baptism carries these meanings because first and fundamentally it signifies union with Christ in his death, burial, and resurrection (Rom 6:3-7; Col 2:11-12); and this union with Christ is the source of every element in our salvation (1 John 5:11-12). Receiving the sign in faith assures the persons baptized that God's gift of new life in Christ is freely given to them" (J. I. Packer, *Concise Theology* [Wheaton, Ill.: Tyndale House, 1993], p. 212).

[35]An excellent and much fuller discussion has been provided by Stephen Wellum. The reader is strongly encouraged to read his treatment with great care. See Stephen J. Wellum, "Baptism and the Relationship Between the Covenants," in *Believer's Baptism: Sign of the New Covenant in Christ,* ed. Thomas R. Schreiner and Shawn D. Wright, New American Commentary Studies in Bible & Theology 2 (Nashville: B & H, 2007), pp. 97-161.

nuity between the old and new covenants (e.g., both covenants call
God's people to live obedient lives, and both are given visible signs
and seals through circumcision and baptism respectively), there is
also significant discontinuity as well.[36]

Within this discussion, it is precisely on the question of what constitutes the *discontinuity* between old and new covenants that the disagreement with paedobaptists arises. Wellum introduces his evalua-
tion and critique of the covenantal argument for paedobaptism with
the following summary observations:

> Central to my critique of the covenantal argument for infant baptism
> is that it fails to understand correctly the proper relationships between
> the biblical covenants and the degree of continuity and discontinuity
> between them. Paedobaptists rightly emphasize the unity and conti-
> nuity of God's salvific plan across the ages. They fail to do justice,
> however, to the progressive nature of God's revelation, especially in
> regard to the biblical covenants, the covenant community, and the
> covenant signs. In the end, this leads them to misunderstand the
> proper degree of discontinuity inaugurated by Christ's coming and to
> which the Old Testament points, namely the arrival of the promised
> new covenant age. . . . What this entails for our reading of Scripture
> and doing theology is that we must do justice to the unity of God's
> plan without flattening the epochal changes that have occurred now
> that the Lord of Glory has ushered in the end of the ages.[37]

---

[36]I write as one who gladly identifies himself as a progressive dispensationalist. I have
defended my own understanding of the nature of the new covenant previously. See
Bruce A. Ware, "The New Covenant and the People(s) of God" in *Dispensationalism,
Israel and the Church: The Search for Definition,* ed. Craig A. Blaising and Darrell L. Bock,
(Grand Rapids: Zondervan, 1992), pp. 68-97. Interestingly, Wellum, "Baptism" pp.
97-161, who presents the superb treatment of the relationship between new and old
covenants and its relevance to baptism cited above, writes as one identified broadly
within the tradition of covenant theology. Although he argues that the "covenant of
grace," as used in covenant theology by paedobaptists, is misleading, he nonetheless
stands self-consciously within this broad and multiform covenant theology tradition.
Despite our differences, then, Wellum and I agree fully that understanding rightly
the discontinuity (as well as continuity, to be sure) between old and new covenants is
crucial both hermeneutically and to a correct understanding of the new covenant and
its sign of baptism.
[37]Wellum, "Baptism," p. 125.

I could not agree more fully. Consider, then, two of the main lines of this discontinuity between the old and new covenants, specifically as these provide grounding to the credobaptist understanding of baptism.

First, and central to any and all other differences, the old covenant incorporated the people of God at two levels, one ethnic and national, and the other spiritual, whereas the new covenant constitutes as the people of God exclusively those who have believed in Christ and have received forgiveness of their sins through his atoning death. There is a sense in which, under the old covenant, all those who descend from the line of Abraham, Isaac and Jacob, are properly speaking the people of God. This is mainly why God forbade his people to intermarry with other ethnic and national peoples. God chose Abraham, and then Isaac (not Ishmael), and then Jacob (not Esau) as the specific line of those who would constitute his own people, and the line through whom the Messiah would come. So ethnic, national Israel, so constituted as a theocracy under the law, was a national people of the one true God.

In another sense, however, only the "remnant" within Israel, that is, those who faithfully followed God and his law, were truly the people of God, spiritually. The true Israel, as it were, was spiritual Israel, those constituted as God's people through a faith and obedience that extended beyond their ethnic-national identity alone.

So the *old covenant people* of God were a mixed company. Ethnically and nationally, they comprised both believing and unbelieving Jews, but spiritually there was the believing remnant who constituted the true or spiritual Israel. The constitution of the *new covenant people* could not be more markedly different, however. Jeremiah 31:31-34 presents this new covenant, describing all new covenant members as law-keeping, obedient people:

> Behold, the days are coming, declares the LORD, when I will make a new covenant with the house of Israel and the house of Judah, not like the covenant that I made with their fathers on the day when I took them by the hand to bring them out of the land of Egypt, my

covenant that they broke, though I was their husband, declares the
LORD. But this is the covenant that I will make with the house of
Israel after those days, declares the LORD: I will put my law within
them, and I will write it on their hearts. And I will be their God, and
they shall be my people. And no longer shall each one teach his
neighbor and each his brother, saying, "Know the LORD," for they
shall all know me, from the least of them to the greatest, declares the
LORD. For I will forgive their iniquity, and I will remember their sin
no more.

Consider three observations from this text. First, this new covenant is "not like" the old covenant, precisely in that God's people
"broke" the old covenant, while this new covenant, by implication,
will not be broken. That is, God will not fail to make all of those in
the new covenant faithful covenant partners.

Second, this is confirmed when we read that God will put his law
"within them" and on their hearts he will "write it." The law, on
tablets of stone under the old covenant, now becomes the law in-
scribed on human hearts, resulting in a law-keeping from the very
(new) natures of these covenant participants (cf. Ezek 36:26-36,
where the Spirit is put within those whose new hearts will keep the
statutes of God).

And third, in the new covenant every single member will "know
the LORD." There is no category for unbelieving covenant members. All new covenant participants will be covenant keepers, will
know and embrace the law intrinsically, and will know the Lord
and be his spiritual people.[38] The two categories of the people of

---

[38]Interestingly, the paedobaptist Pratt, "Infant Baptism in the New Covenant," pp.
160-61, agrees that the new covenant comprises exclusively believers. Of Jer 31:31-34,
he writes, "In a word, to know God as Jeremiah spoke of it would be to receive eternal
salvation. In the covenant of which Jeremiah spoke, salvation would come to each
participant. There would be no exceptions." I could not agree more fully. So how does
Pratt, then, continue to understand infant baptism as appropriate in the new covenant?
His answer essentially appeals to the progressive nature of the fulfillment of the new
covenant, in which people are not brought to faith and full obedience immediately.
There is an "already" and "not yet" to new covenant reality. Therefore, he asserts,
"Consequently, there is no need to withhold baptism from infants on the basis of Jer-

God under the old covenant, then, gives way to one solitary category under the new.

Second, the sign of the old covenant, circumcision, functioned at two levels, one corresponding to the people of God in their physical descent as the ethnic and national people of Israel, and the other corresponding to the true and spiritual Israel, as those who had circumcised hearts before God. This explains why in Romans 4:11 Paul can refer to circumcision as a sign and seal of faith since it functioned both physically to mark off the ethnic descendants of Abraham and spiritually to signify those of faith and trust in God. In contrast the new covenant pertains exclusively to one people of God: those who have believed in Christ and have received forgiveness of their sins through his atoning death. Therefore the sign of the new covenant, baptism, applies only to believers. Precisely because the people of God under the new covenant are, in their entirety, those of faith and trust in God through Christ, it is therefore right to apply baptism as the sign of their new life in Christ only to them. Wellum writes:

> In the OT era, the people of God were both a nation and the spiritual people of God; circumcision signaled one's affiliation with the nation. But even though circumcision marked one as a *natural* seed of Abraham and brought one into the nation of Israel, not all who were part of Israel were the *spiritual* seed (see Rom 9:6). This . . . is *not* the same in regard to the new covenant people of God. The new covenant people of God are all those, regardless of ethnicity or circumci-

---

emiah's new covenant expectations. Until the consummation, the new covenant will continue to be a mixture of true believers and sanctified unbelievers" (idem, p. 173). The main problem with this reading is that, even if the fulfillment of the new covenant reality of faith and obedience takes place progressively (which surely it does), still, *all* of those in the new covenant are believers. But if infants are baptized who never come to faith and obedience, they have then wrongly received the sign of the new covenant. The only way in which we can rightly and truly apply the sign of the new covenant is as we apply it to professing believers. How can we rightly apply the sign of the covenant to infants who, by nature and necessity, are not even in the "already" of the salvation experience which their baptism supposedly signifies? Hence believers' baptism alone is consistent with the new covenant, whose constitutive membership is (as Pratt acknowledges) exclusively believers.

sion, who have confessed Christ as Lord, the *true/spiritual* seed of Abraham. Thus it includes all those who believe in Christ and who have been born of his Spirit. That is why, in the end, Scripture teaches that we should only baptize those who are Christ's covenant children—those who are actually in the covenant by God's grace through regeneration and saving faith.[39]

The new covenant people of God are made up of men and women, boys and girls, from every tribe, tongue, people and nation who share in common their faith and trust in Christ alone for their salvation. They include, then, both circumcised and uncircumcised believers, and this point is of no little significance for our discussion. For Paul in particular, the fact that both Jews and Gentiles are brought into one body through faith in Christ required that circumcision be set aside as a marker for the people of God (cf. 1 Cor 7:18-19; Gal 5:1-11; Eph 2:11-22). No physical marker of ethnic descent would be appropriate any longer. The parallel, then, between circumcision and baptism in the new covenant is not between physical circumcision and infant baptism; rather, the parallel is between spiritual circumcision of the heart and baptism which signifies regeneration, faith and union with Christ (cf. Col 2:11-12).

Indeed, as many Baptists have pointed out, if New Testament writers genuinely saw a parallel between physical circumcision and infant baptism, it is utterly remarkable that they never said so in the New Testament.[40] Certainly, with as much complaint as the apostles received from the Judaizers over discarding circumcision, the most natural and compelling response would have been to say that infant baptism now carries forward the same significance in the new covenant that circumcision did under the old covenant. But this point is

---

[39]Wellum, "Baptism," p. 136. See also Jewett, *Infant Baptism and the Covenant of Grace,* pp. 93-104; Malone, *Baptism of Disciples Alone,* pp. 71-79.

[40]In an excellent sermon, "How do Circumcision and Baptism Correspond?" preached at Bethlehem Baptist Church, Minneapolis, Minn., August 29, 1999, John Piper makes this point, appealing especially to Acts 15 as the most likely place we would find in the NT where infant baptism would naturally be raised; but alas it is not. Piper's sermon may be accessed at <www.desiringgod.org/ResourceLibrary/Sermons>.

never made. Instead physical circumcision is rejected as unnecessary,
and spiritual circumcision is fulfilled and shown as parallel to baptism, which is administered exclusively to those who have trusted in
Christ for their salvation. Because the new covenant envisions a
company of believers and only believers, the sign of the new covenant, baptism, is rightly administered only to those who are members of the new covenant by faith in Christ.[41]

HISTORICAL SUPPORT FOR BELIEVERS' BAPTISM

Despite some popular opinion to the contrary, a growing body of
scholarship is demonstrating that believers' baptism was the belief
and practice of the church for the first four centuries. Stander and
Louw's historical study[42] documents over and over again how statements from early church writers about the baptism of "children" are
taken by paedobaptists to indicate that infant baptism was practiced.
But in fact, as one examines the contexts of these statements, one
often finds that the "children" spoken of are said to believe or ask
questions or in some way indicate that they are well beyond infancy.
For example, they comment how some paedobaptists cite a statement
from Justin Martyr (ca. A.D. 100-165) as supporting infant baptism.
The statement from Justin reads, "There are among us many, both
men and women, who have been Christ's disciples from childhood,

---

[41]Critics of paedobaptism also rightly observe some aspects of the old covenant which
don't seem to find an echo in new covenant living for those who practice infant baptism: (1) circumcision was of infant males only, but infant baptism is performed on
infant boys and girls, and (2) young children of the old covenant participated in the
annual celebration of the Passover meal, yet typically young children, who were baptized as infants but who have not confessed personal faith in Christ, are not permitted
to partake of the elements at the Lord's Table. Interestingly on this latter point the
paedobaptist Jerram Barrs argues against paedocommunion precisely because the New
Testament indicates *discontinuity* with the old covenant on this point. He appeals to
1 Cor 11:27-29, where Paul requires that those who eat of the Lord's Table first discern
the body and blood of the Lord, which infants cannot do. If paedobaptists would only
take their cues from the New Testament regarding baptism in the manner Barrs does
for the Lord's Table, we would be on our way toward reconciliation! Barrs's comments on this subject may be accessed at <www.covenantseminary.edu/worldwide/
en/PT330/PT330.asp> (Worship course, Lecture 20).
[42]Stander and Louw, *Baptism in the Early Church*.

and who remain pure at the age of sixty or seventy years."[43] In response Stander and Louw demonstrate that the phrase translated "from childhood" can refer to the early years of a person's life up to their being sixteen to eighteen years of age. Furthermore what others sometimes fail to mention when Justin's statement is quoted in support of infant baptism is that "there are a number of explicit descriptions of the nature of baptism, namely believer's baptism, in this same work of Justin" from which this quotation is taken.[44] After quoting a lengthy passage from Justin where he describes his view of baptism in some detail, Stander and Louw provide the following summation:

> In this passage [Justin's *Apology* 61, 65] Justin clearly spells out what the Church of his time required from a person before he was accepted for baptism: firstly, the person had to believe in the truth of the Christian doctrine; secondly, he had to undertake to live accordingly; thirdly, the baptismal candidate had to undergo a period of devotion and fasting in which he had to request God to forgive all his past sins. . . . Since only mature persons could satisfy these preconditions, it undoubtedly excludes the possibility that infants were involved in these activities.[45]

Examples like this one are given throughout Stander and Louw's study demonstrating that infant baptism did not develop in any significant way until the fourth century. When it did, it tended to grow in acceptance among Christian people along with a growing belief that baptism itself was necessary for the remission of sins. Hence, as the conviction developed that through infant baptism the subject baptized would be forgiven, the advocacy and practice of infant baptism increased.[46] Stander and Louw conclude their historical study as follows:

---

[43]Justin Martyr *First Apology*, as quoted in Stander and Louw, *Baptism in the Early Church*, p. 4.

[44]Stander and Louw, *Baptism in the Early Church*, p. 4.

[45]Ibid., p. 24.

[46]Ibid., pp. 117-21.

In the first four centuries of Christianity, the literature on baptism clearly shows how, in the majority of instances, it was persons of responsible age (generally adults and grown children) who were the recipients of baptism. Emergency baptism and the eventual linking of baptism to circumcision, as well as the fact that baptism was believed to remove sin, occasioned the extension of baptism to small children and finally to infants. Though some authors (Tertullian and Gregory of Nazianzus) opposed this development, others (Cyprian) strongly advocated this trend. . . . The rite of baptism itself, rather than Christ, became the guarantee of eternal salvation.[47]

Other historians have come to similar conclusions. David Wright goes even further than Stander and Louw when he states, "The baptismal experience of the church of the early Fathers was largely of believer's baptism, or perhaps better conversion baptism. Historical study is steadily consolidating the conclusion that infant baptism did not really come into its own, as the common practice, until after Augustine, perhaps in the sixth century."[48] So while it is the case that infant baptism has been practiced by many branches of the church, and for many centuries, the conclusions of recent scholarship are that believers' baptism was the conviction and practice for the first four to six centuries of the church as it was of the New Testament church itself.

COMMENDING BELIEVERS' BAPTISM

Consider two concluding reasons to commend believers' baptism for the health and well-being of the church. First, the practice of credobaptism has the potential of providing a young Christian a wonderful and sacred opportunity to certify personally and testify publicly of his own identity, now, as a follower of Christ. How rich and meaningful believers' baptism is!

What a wonderful opportunity is afforded one who has confessed

---

[47]Ibid., p. 119.

[48]David F. Wright, "Recovering Baptism for a New Age of Mission," in *Doing Theology for the People of God: Studies in Honor of J. I. Packer,* ed. Donald Lewis and Alister McGrath (Downers Grove, Ill.: InterVarsity Press, 1996), p. 57.

Christ as his Savior and Lord now to declare his allegiance to Christ through his immersion into the waters of baptism (1 Pet 3:21). As he goes under the water and rises cleansed and renewed, he pictures to others outwardly the reality of his own inner spiritual death to his old life and his new and resurrected life in Christ (Rom 6:3-11). The practice of believers' baptism, then, is a precious gift to offer any and every believer in Jesus Christ, since it marks one off clearly and exclusively as belonging wholly to Christ. Obedience to Christ matters. Since Christ commanded his followers to be baptized, and since baptism in the New Testament is believers' baptism, obedience to Christ requires that all true believers be baptized following their own personal faith in Christ for their salvation.

Second, the practice of credobaptism grounds the regenerate membership of the church. One of the great problems and frustrations connected with paedobaptism is that it continues necessarily the "mixed" company of the church in a way that parallels the "mixed" company within Israel. If membership in the new covenant and hence in the church comes via infant baptism, yet salvation comes only by faith, then it follows that paedobaptist churches are necessarily afflicted with the problem of a potentially significant number of unregenerate church members. Of course believers' baptism is no guarantee that every church member is truly saved, to be sure. But at least *in principle* and *by structure and design*, a church that adheres to believers' baptism and upholds this baptism as prerequisite for church membership, since obedience to Christ requires believers' baptism, such a church consciously seeks to maintain a fully regenerate church membership. This practice, then, will only enhance the health and well-being of local churches. For the honor of Christ, for the obedience of his people, for the witness of Christ before a watching world, and for the health and purity of the church, let us commit ourselves to seek afresh to know and follow Scripture's teaching on the nature and practice of baptism.

INFANT BAPTISM RESPONSE

Sinclair B. Ferguson

PROFESSOR BRUCE WARE HAS GIVEN a vigorous apologia for credobaptism, forcefully stating his conclusion: paedobaptists "are living in disobedience to Christ" (p. 20). It is impossible here to respond with exegetical detail to all the points Dr. Ware makes, but several comments may be made.

BAPTISM BY IMMERSION

Dr. Ware argues that "the term *baptism* refers most clearly and naturally to the immersion of a person in water." Some noted paedobaptists have also held this view, not least John Calvin.[1] Four things, should however be noted:

1. The New Testament *accounts* of baptism neither indicate nor require immersion as the mode except when they are read through an a priori lens. Were baptism by affusion (pouring), it would not require the rewording of any of the relevant passages (e.g., Mt 3:16; Mk 1:10; Acts 8:38).

A similar comment can be made of the teaching of *Didache* 7:

> Baptize "in the name of the Father and the Son and the Holy Spirit" in running water. But if you have no running water, then baptize

---

[1]John Calvin *Institutes of the Christian Religion* 4.15.19.

in some other water; and if you are not able to baptize in cold water, then do so warm. But if you have neither, then pour water on the head three times, "in the name of Father and Son and Holy Spirit."[2]

The symbolism here is the washing away of sin. I suspect the *Didache* itself may have been misread at this point as though baptism in running water, other water, cold water, warm water, by pouring water on the head three times were *a series of alternative modes*. Rather they are *a series of different contexts*. The *only mode* mentioned is affusion.

2. New Testament *expositions* of baptism do not require immersion. These characteristically relate baptism to union with Christ in his death and resurrection. To imply that immersion alone represents this presupposes a Western concept of burial. Nor is our Lord's death (being "lifted up" on the cross) particularly well symbolized in immersion, nor even the mode of his burial (in a tomb, not under the earth).

3. The *root* meaning of *baptō/baptizō* is not immersion as such. Most fundamentally it seems to express the idea of one thing being overwhelmed by another. Immersion may express this, but it has no exclusive claim to do so, as examples from classical literature indicate. Indeed in the New Testament rather than mean "immerse," the verb *baptizein* means "baptize."

4. In this context the New Testament features one highly significant baptism. The mode of the baptism that fulfills our Lord's promise "you will be baptized with the Holy Spirit" (Acts 1:5; cf. Mt 3:11 and parallels) was *pouring* (*echeō*, Acts 2:17, 33; used also of the Spirit in Rom. 5:5). It is therefore impossible exegetically to insist that baptism *means* to immerse. Indeed this fundamental baptism presents a case for affusion as the mode used in the early church (cf. *Didache* 7). After all, it is the outpouring of the Spirit that effects that union with Christ in his death and resurrection in which we are justified and sanctified.

---

[2]*Didache* 7.1-3 (*AF*, p. 259).

Dr. Ware believes the argument *for immersion* is simultaneously an argument *against the baptism of infants:* "as such, its very usage argues directly for immersion as the mode of baptism, and indirectly for the application of baptism to those past infancy" (p. 21).

This is special pleading. The first Christians were used to an initiation rite in which they watched (and some actually performed) the cutting off of the foreskin of their eight-day-old sons! Even if baptism were immersion, it is unlikely that such fathers would have qualms about a momentary submersion of their infants!

Furthermore Dr. Ware dismisses the Orthodox practice of baptism as virtually irrelevant (p. 23 n. 14). Yet it and other paedobaptist churches who practice immersion constitute a massive counter argument to his case. I confess a vested interest here. Were I to write "My wife was baptized as an infant," a reader might conclude she could not have been immersed. Were I to write "My wife was baptized by immersion," another reader might conclude she could not have been baptized as an infant. Both would be wrong. Yet another might assume she was Eastern Orthodox. But no. The use of the verb "baptize" disclosed nothing about the mode. The assumptions about the mode were in the minds of my hearers not in the meaning of the term. So also in the New Testament.

MEANING OF BAPTISM

Why do credobaptists and paedobaptists disagree on the subjects of baptism?

From one perspective paedobaptists appear to disagree *only in part* with credobaptists. One of the joys of being a paedobaptist is that we baptize those from outside of the church who have been drawn to a living faith in Christ. We too have our stories of such baptisms and their impact. The obverse is not the case. Dr. Ware's doctrine allows neither the baptism of infants nor, presumably, their belonging (in any biblically explicable and theologically coherent sense) to the church as the family of God.

But why say that paedobaptists *appear* to disagree only in part?

Here we come to a major fault line. We not only hold to different modes and subjects; characteristically, we operate with different definitions. In this respect Professor Ware's quotation (p. 41 n. 34) of J. I. Packer's "definition of baptism" is intriguing:

> Christian baptism . . . is a sign from God that signifies inward cleansing and remission of sins, . . . Spirit-wrought regeneration and new life, . . . and the abiding presence of the Holy Spirit as God's seal testifying and guaranteeing that one will be kept safe in Christ forever. . . . Baptism carries these meanings because first and fundamentally it signifies union with Christ in his death, burial and resurrection . . . and this union with Christ is the source of every element in our salvation. . . . Receiving the sign in faith assures the baptized that God's gift of new life in Christ is freely given to them.[3]

Dr. Ware describes it as "a definition . . . any Baptist would relish" (p. 41 n. 34). Would that it were so! Dr. Packer's definition describes the objective significance of baptism as a sign of Jesus Christ clothed in the garments of the gospel to be received and enjoyed in faith. But this actually contrasts sharply with, for example, the Faith and Message statement adopted by the Southern Baptist Church in its annual meeting in 2000:

> Christian baptism is the immersion of a believer in water in the name of the Father, the Son, and the Holy Spirit. *It is an act of obedience symbolizing the believer's faith* in a crucified, buried, and risen Savior, the believer's death to sin, the burial of the old life, and the resurrection to walk in newness of life in Christ Jesus. *It is a testimony to his faith* in the final resurrection of the dead.[4]

This definition offers a significantly different perspective on baptism. The same element (water, in varying amounts) and the same formula (Trinity) are used. However, not only the subjects but also *the very meaning of the sign* is different. For the credobaptist, typically,

---

[3]J. I. Packer, *Concise Theology* (Wheaton, Ill.: Tyndale House, 1993), p. 212.
[4]Section 7, "Baptism and the Lord's Supper," *Baptist Faith and Message,* 2000 edition (emphasis mine).

baptism is a sign of *what the believer has done* in response to Christ; for the paedobaptist, baptism is first a sign of *what Christ has done,* and of all that is in him to be received in faith. If "any Baptist would relish" Dr. Packer's definition, I suspect he or she is out of step with the confessional statement of possibly the largest association of credo-baptists in the world!

Professor Ware is (sadly), therefore, overly sanguine (p. 41) in finding agreement between "most credobaptists and paedobaptists," that "baptism is the sign and seal of the new covenant." In fact the great historic London (1689) and Philadelphia (1742) Baptist Confessions, demonstrably modeled on the Westminster Confession, deliberately deleted this language.

Dr. Ware's further exposition seems to me to return to the basic gestalt of the Southern Baptist Convention Statement of Faith, where what is fundamentally signified is the subjective response of faith, not the objective Christ of the New Covenant.

This inevitably tints the lens through which the New Testament and its relationship to the Old Testament revelation are read. One—significant—illustration of this is that Professor Ware speaks of the way in which "in Romans 4:11, Paul can refer to circumcision as a sign and seal of faith" (p. 45). But this is *not* what Paul says. Rather he affirms that "he [Abraham] received the sign of circumcision as a seal *of the righteousness* that he had *by faith*" (Rom 4:11 NRSV, my emphasis). Like all covenant signs, circumcision signified the divine activity and grace to which recipients were called to respond in faith (cf. Gen 17:11). It did not signify faith itself.

This perspectival difference in understanding what baptism signifies inevitably has a significant effect on the way in which the text of Scripture will be exegeted. In that respect the following comments are offered on specific points in Dr. Ware's exegesis. We can do little more than briefly indicate lines of response.

EXEGESIS

Matthew 28:18-20. Two points are worth making. These words, like

much of the New Testament, are set in the context of the first proclamation of the gospel to the world. Unsurprisingly the focus is on
the baptism of those who hear and believe in Christ. It is no embar-
rassment to paedobaptist theology or practice that this is the case.

But Dr. Ware feels the need to close an exegetical gap: "make disciples," "baptizing" and "teaching" "seems to indicate that those baptized are also able to be taught" (p. 24). Indeed—but by no necessary
exegesis does the teaching require to be synchronized with baptism.
The expectation to teach is satisfied when parents fulfill their vows to
"teach your child the truths and duties of the Christian faith, and by
prayer, precept and example, bring them up in the nurture and admonition of the Lord and the ways of the church of God." To insist on the
simultaneity of the baptizing and teaching is to see the text with credobaptist eyes and to read more into it than can be read out of it.

A similar insistence is reflected in Dr. Ware's citation (from
Thomas R. Schreiner[5]) that "it is difficult to see how the reception
of the Spirit could be predicated of infants since the Spirit is received
by faith" (p. 28). If so, infant salvation surely is impossible, and it is
difficult to know what to make of the Spirit's work on the humanity
of our Lord and his forerunner John while each was in his mother's
womb (Lk 1:15, 35).

Household baptisms. Dr. Ware seeks to counter at length the paedobaptist contention (sometimes also lengthy!) that household baptisms
may have included infants. Acts 16:29-34 is a minefield in this
regard.

By definition a "household" included infants, if there were any.
Dr. Ware again seeks to close textual "gaps" to insist that only those
converted were baptized. The text may not be amenable to a logically watertight(!) position. The use of the concept "household" itself, however, bespeaks a deep continuity between Old and New

---

[5]Thomas R. Schreiner, "Baptism in the Epistles: An Initiation Rite for Believers," in *Be-
liever's Baptism: Sign of the New Covenant in Christ,* ed. Thomas R. Schreiner and Shawn
D. Wright, New American Commentary Studies in Bible & Theology 2 (Nashville:
B & H, 2007), p. 93.

Testament covenantal understanding of the family before God—with all that this entailed in faith and expectation.

The "promise" of Pentecost. Credobaptist exegesis characteristically insists that "promise" in Acts 2:39 be limited to the immediate antecedent, "the Holy Spirit." Professor Ware is more generous in that he is willing to say that "all that is happening at this time . . . relates directly to the fulfillment of God's original promise to Abraham" (p. 35).

I applaud Dr. Ware's concern to bring credobaptist theology back to reformed roots and a covenantal theology. But here again he seems to revert to credobaptist type and abstracts Peter's words from their context in his sermon, his use of Scripture, and the biblical story of the "promise"—whose deep biblical-theological and redemptive-historical echoes would have been grasped by Peter's hearers.

Peter's words underscore the principle of covenant continuity and do so just where Dr. Ware shares S. J. Wellum's[6] complaint that paedobaptists' covenantal thought "fails to understand correctly the proper relationships between the biblical covenants," and they "misunderstand the proper degree of discontinuity" (p. 42). Peter's words "for you *and your children* and for all who are far off" (Acts 2:39 NIV, my emphasis) underline the principle of continuity, as well as of advance ("far off" being biblical language for Gentiles, Eph 2:13). Had Peter believed in a discontinuity (i.e., if Peter were a credobaptist!), he would have been wise to avoid saying "and your children." He supplies this middle term and thus explicitly expresses continuity. It is in vain here to appeal to the words "everyone whom the Lord our God calls to himself" (Acts 2:39) as if this were a new covenant novelty. God's promise had always been activated by calling!

The promise of the new covenant (Jer 31:31-34). It must suffice here to point out, against Dr. Ware (pp. 43-44), that Jeremiah did see the

---

[6]Stephen J. Wellum, "The Believer's Baptism: Relationships Between the Covenants," in *Believer's Baptism: Sign of the New Covenant in Christ,* ed. Thomas R. Schreiner and Shawn D. Wright, New American Commentary Studies in Bible & Theology 2 (Nashville: B & H, 2007), p. 125.

"to you and your seed" covenant principle continuing into the future (cf. Jer 32:38-40). Furthermore this covenant principle preceded the Mosaic administration, whose abrogation Jeremiah prophesies (credobaptist exegesis often misses this, and with it the undergirding of the text). Unsurprisingly then the "and your seed" principle survives the abrogation of the Mosaic economy. This cannot here be expounded at length, but it is fundamental to Peter's understanding of Joel 2:18—3:1 and to the use of Jeremiah 31:31-34 in Hebrews 8 and 10.

THE RELATIONSHIP BETWEEN CIRCUMCISION AND BAPTISM

Dr. Ware denies that baptism replaces circumcision. He seeks to do this in his exegesis of Colossians 2:11-15. This he holds is further demonstrated by the fact that neither the Council of Jerusalem nor apostolic teaching rejected the Judaizers' insistence on circumcision by an appeal to baptism as its replacement.

Paul's concern in Colossians 2:11-15 is to point to the significance of the work of Christ which simultaneously fulfills the meaning of circumcision and grounds the meaning of baptism. In that sense the two signs, each within its own covenant, point to one and the same reality. Since circumcision ceases and baptism continues, the replacement of the former by the latter is a de facto reality. Some credobaptists have acknowledged this and grasped that Paul sees circumcision and baptism as coalescing within the context of progressive revelation in its climax at the cross, where Christ's circumcision and baptism were both realized.

Furthermore the Council of Jerusalem could not have solved the theological problem by saying "Baptism replaces circumcision." The sickness was far deeper, and such a statement would have provided no remedy. For the Judaizers were falling away from the free grace of the gospel. The real problem with "Judaizers" in every age (as the magisterial Reformers of the sixteenth century also saw) is that they misunderstand the grace of the cross of Christ and the new creation—not to mention Old Testament redemptive history (cf. Gal 3:1, 6-29; 6:14-15). The hesitancy of the church shows—alas—that one can replace circumcision with baptism yet retain the theology of the Judaizers.

Two further general points should be noted. From Genesis 17:1-14 through Romans 4:11-12, circumcision was a physical sign of God's covenant, with all its blessings—first of all in relation to God himself ("to be God to you," Gen 17:7) and then in relationship to the present form of his covenant community. In credobaptist polemic, circumcision often becomes first and foremost a sign of ethnic, national, physical blessing. This fails both to grasp the basic dynamics of God's covenants and to see the exegetical and redemptive-historical insight of Paul's words in Romans 4:11-12.

PRACTICAL VALUE

Professor Ware sees great practical value in the baptism of believers only. Paedobaptists see practical value in both the baptism of new converts and the baptism of their children. I have a concern and two questions here.

The concern is that if one applied the underlying principles of some credobaptist arguments one would also become a credo-circumcisionist.

The first question concerns the credobaptist conviction that God no longer has a promise to believers and their children. If so the believing parent today *lacks* what his Old Testament counterpart enjoyed—a gracious promise to faith with respect to children in relationship to God's covenant. As a Calvinistic credobaptist, Professor Ware shares the paedobaptist conviction that nothing in my flesh as a parent gives me any hope for my children's salvation. (Note that this was also the conviction of the right-thinking old-covenant, paedocircumcisionist believer too!) Is it now the intention of the God who reveals the fullness of grace in Christ to remove this hope in the new covenant? This puts the new covenant parent in a position of *regress* from the older covenant.

My concern here is that this represents a view of grace, family and of the Father himself that does not accord well with the New Testament. It fits ill with progressive and epochal advance in the revelation of God and the manifestation of his fullness in Christ. It suggests the Father has withdrawn what he once *generously* gave. It is also a strange Fatherhood that *removes* from his children the basis on which they can pray with the anticipation of covenantal and Christ-centered faith: "Lord, here are my children; I love them, I rest on your promise that you will be their God as well as mine. And I commit myself to all the attendant responsibilities you lay upon me."

The second question is this. What language do we encourage our children to use in relation to God? The (paedobaptist) covenantal principle enables parents to teach their children in home, Sunday School and congregational worship to pray *with theological consistency* "Our Father in heaven . . ." Can a credobaptist do that *with theological consistency?* I doubt it. Thankfully I suspect most credobaptists do. Despite the polemics, we often instinctively do what our intellectual system poorly, if at all, supports. In that respect there is "one baptism."

DUAL-PRACTICE
BAPTISM RESPONSE

Anthony N. S. Lane

BRUCE WARE CONCLUDES HIS THOROUGH PRESENTATION of the Baptist view with a prayer that would be echoed by both Sinclair Ferguson and myself. We are indeed all committed to "know and follow Scripture's teaching on the nature and practice of baptism" (p. 50). But what precisely does Scripture teach on this issue?

IMMERSION

Bruce Ware argues not just for believers' baptism but for "believers' baptism by immersion." I made no mention of the mode of baptism in my essay because it is a separate issue and one that I consider of minor importance. I will confine myself to four brief observations.

First, while it is true that the basic root meaning of the Greek words for baptize and baptism is immerse/immersion, it is not true that the words can simply be reduced to this meaning. Mark 10:38-39 and Luke 12:50 do not refer to a literal immersion into anything. Is immersion in fire the meaning in Matthew 3:11/Luke 3:16? Was Israel immersed in Moses (1 Cor 10:2)?

Second, I do agree immersion was probably the normal practice of baptism.

Third, the mode of baptism was not in the early church regarded as an important issue. The *Didache*, quite likely the oldest Christian writing outside the New Testament, gives instruction that if there is insufficient water one should pour water on the head of the candidate three times, in the name of the Father and of the Son and of the Holy Spirit.[1] Nothing hints that this made the baptism any less valid. Where the early church was much clearer was in the practice of *threefold* baptism, in the name of the Trinity.

Finally, this matter is of limited relevance to our present debate since, as Bruce Ware notes (p. 23 n. 14) the Orthodox churches baptize infants by immersion. Indeed David Wright tells us that "Boris Yeltsin was nearly drowned by a tipsy priest when being baptized in a Siberian village as a child"![2]

THE NEW TESTAMENT NORM

The majority of Bruce Ware's essay is, quite rightly, devoted to expounding the New Testament. What does he establish? He argues that the pattern of baptism presented in the New Testament is believers' baptism. But the New Testament norm is not so much believers' baptism as converts' baptism—the baptism of people not at some random stage after they come to faith but specifically at the point where they come to faith.[3] Integral to this is the fact that, according to Acts, coming to faith and baptism occurred at the same time. For good or ill, that is something that happens rarely in the Christian West today. It is also something that does not normally happen to those raised in a Christian home—though I suppose one might take care to isolate one's children from all exposure to the Christian faith and then, when they reach the right age, proclaim it to them in the hope that they will at once repent, believe, be baptized and receive the Spirit! So while the normative pattern in the

---

[1] *Didache* 7.
[2] "Baptism at the Westminster Assembly," in *The Westminster Confession in Current Thought,* ed. J. H. Leith, Calvin Studies 8 (Davidson, N.C.: Davidson College, 1996), p. 84.
[3] George R. Beasley-Murray, *Baptism in the New Testament* (London: Macmillan, 1962), e.g., pp. 393-94.

New Testament is converts' baptism, this will need to be adjusted to fit the circumstances of those whose initiation into the Christian faith is not so immediate. Subsequent baptism when an individual reaches the age of maturity/adulthood is *one* way of making this adjustment.

In addition to arguing that the New Testament narrates and assumes believers' baptism (which we may concede with the qualification that it teaches the baptism of believing *converts*), Bruce Ware seeks to show that the New Testament does not allow for the baptism of children too young to believe. "The New Testament also offers no clear and unmistakable instance of nonbelievers' or infant baptism" (p. 29). This statement is correct in that no passage in the New Testament *clearly and unmistakably* describes the baptism of an infant.

I would respond that at least some events, the household baptisms, may be understood to include the baptism of infants. Perhaps some passages may reasonably and plausibly be taken to do so? Where the household baptisms are concerned, Ware ably demonstrates that they do not *have* to imply the baptism of any infants. In no case is there "specific mention that infants were among those in the household who were baptized" (p. 34). True, but that does not prove that there were none. By contrast we have no evidence whatsoever for the baptism at a later date of a child born into a Christian family.

At this point the worldview of the commentator becomes important. Bruce Ware writes from the stance of modern Western individualism. He considers it inconceivable that the head of a household might make decisions for other members of the household. For the modern Westerner we are all individuals who must make our own decisions for ourselves—what career we will pursue, whom we will marry, what religion we will follow. This is self-evident to us. It is not so self-evident to other cultures, and it is anachronistic to suppose that the first-century Christians thought that way. It is not a coincidence that the *principled rejection* of infant baptism, the belief that it is wrong, originated in the sixteenth century, at a time when individualism was becoming stronger in the West. Why is it that no one read the New Testament that way for three quarters of the church's history?

The reverse side of this is that the Baptist strategy (i.e., non-baptism of babies) may well be defended as a good way to contextualize baptism in a modern individualistic culture, where it is less acceptable for parents to make decisions for their children—though paedobaptists might regard this as a sell-out to modern culture. If, as I have argued, the apostolic pattern of diversity of practice is the only one for which the early centuries offer any clear evidence, then the church has room for a legitimate variety of views and of practice on this issue.

For paedobaptists the problem is *inconclusive* evidence that it happened in the first 150 years of the church; for Baptists the problem is *total lack* of evidence that their pattern was followed. No record before the third century speaks of the later baptism of a child from a Christian home, and no hint appears in the epistles that such children should be seeking baptism. What we have is nearly complete silence about what happened to children born into Christian homes. Baptists have at times cleverly exploited this as if it were a silence about infant baptism only, which it is not.

THE EFFICACY OF BAPTISM

At one point Bruce Ware states that "baptism which expresses an appeal to God for forgiveness, through the death and resurrection of Christ, is salvific" (p. 28). Elsewhere he sees baptism rather as a sign of what has *already* happened. "The sign of baptism corresponds to the reality of spiritual conversion that has already taken place in their lives" (p. 28). "For the sign (baptism) to be administered, the reality (new life in Christ by faith) must have first taken place" (p. 29). Where in Acts 2:38 Peter exhorts his hearers to "repent and *be baptized* every one of you in the name of Jesus Christ for the forgiveness of your sins, and you will receive the gift of the Holy Spirit" (Acts 2:38, emphasis mine), "clearly what Peter means here is . . . the promise of receiving the indwelling Holy Spirit through repentance and *faith in Christ*" (p. 37, my emphasis). Despite the first sentence quoted above, it appears that Bruce Ware sees baptism as a sign of realities that have already been appropriated. This is a well-established Baptist tradition. The Baptist theologian A. H. Strong illustrated this view with an unfortunate analogy, describing baptism as a symbol of an already existing union, like a wedding service.[4] While this analogy might make sense in an age where many couples cohabit before getting married, that is hardly what Strong, writing a hundred years ago, had in mind! The whole point about a wedding is that it is *not* meant to be a symbol of an already existing union. Two individuals enter as single people and emerge as a married couple. A wedding is not just symbolic of an already existing union but itself creates a new form of union. The same is true of baptism. Strong states that baptism signifies our existing union with Christ in his death and resurrection; Paul states that this union takes place by baptism (Rom 6:3-4; Col 2:12).

The tradition represented by Strong and Ware has been and remains the majority Baptist tradition, but an alternative tradition takes baptism seriously as an effective instrument. George Beasley-Murray argues forcefully for this tradition in his magisterial *Baptism in the New Testament*,[5] while the Baptist theologian Stanley Grenz is a bit more tentative.[6] Other Baptists have supported this view over the centuries.[7]

The New Testament portrays baptism not just as a symbol pointing to something but as itself having a role in the reception of salvation. If the "pure symbolists" are right a number of New Testament passages will need to be rewritten from the NIV as follows:

Peter replied, "Repent, and believe, every one of you, in the name of

---

[4]A. H. Strong, *Systematic Theology* (1906; London: Pickering & Inglis, n.d.), p. 946.
[5]Beasley-Murray, *Baptism in the New Testament*.
[6]Stanley Grenz, *Theology for the Community of God* (Carlisle, U.K.: Paternoster, 1994), pp. 684-85.
[7]For details see Stanley K. Fowler, *More Than a Symbol: The British Baptist Recovery of Baptismal Sacramentalism*, Studies in Baptist History and Thought 2 (Carlisle, U.K.: Paternoster, 2002).

Jesus Christ for the forgiveness of your sins. And you will receive the
gift of the Holy Spirit. You should then be baptized as a sign of this."
(Acts 2:38)

And now what are you waiting for? Get up, be baptized and testify
that your sins have already been washed away, when you called on his
name. (Acts 22:16)

So you are all sons of God through faith in Christ Jesus and have
clothed yourselves with Christ. It was to testify to this that you were
all baptized. (Gal 3:26-27)

This water baptism is a symbol that you have been saved. (1 Pet
3:21)

The New Testament portrays baptism (not in isolation but together with faith) as the means by which we receive the gift of salvation, including forgiveness, union with Christ and the Holy Spirit.[8]
This coheres with the pattern of fourfold initiation that I describe in
my main essay, whereby becoming a Christian involves repentance,
faith, baptism and reception of the Holy Spirit. Because (as we see in
Acts) these all came together the New Testament writers were not
embarrassed to attribute salvation to baptism as well as to faith. Salvation is received by the faith that expresses itself in baptism and by
the baptism that is an expression of faith. Of course attributing this
power to baptism separate from faith is an abuse of the New Testament. The New Testament attributes efficacy to believing baptism,
not to unbelieving baptism. But to attribute efficacy to faith in isolation from baptism is just as surely an abuse of the New Testament.

Given the high view of baptism found in the New Testament,
what is the significance of infant baptism? Are babies born again
in baptism since baptism is (I would argue) associated with regeneration in John 3:5[9] and Titus 3:5? In the New Testament we

---

[8]As is expounded by Beasley-Murray, *Baptism in the New Testament*, pp. 263-305, on the
  basis of the preceding exegetical work (pp. 93-262).
[9]Certainly the Christians of the first few centuries consistently and repeatedly refer this
  verse to baptism.

become Christians by repenting, believing, being baptized and receiving the Spirit. In this fourfold manner we become Christians, not by a faith that is devoid of the others and certainly not by baptism on its own. The aim of parents for their children should be to lead them to full Christian initiation involving believing, repenting, being baptized and receiving the Spirit. Whether baptism comes at the beginning of that process as its commencement or at the end as its culmination is a secondary issue and one on which the early church (including, I have argued, the apostolic church) was happy to allow variety.

Does this high view of baptism mean that salvation cannot occur without baptism? What about the thief on the cross (Lk 23:42-43)?[10] While Mark 16:16 states that "whoever believes and is baptized will be saved," it continues, "whoever does not believe will be condemned"[11] (NIV). Baptism is not put on the same level as faith. That does not give us the liberty to dispense with it. To consider those who, like the thief on the cross, *cannot* be baptized is one thing; to consider those who *will not* be baptized, who refuse baptism, is quite another matter. We must not treat baptism as an optional extra. When people asked to become Christians the apostles did not respond, "Will that be with or without baptism, sir?"

As a Reformed-Baptist dialogue document puts it, "We can set no limits to the power of Christ: he is leading men to salvation in his own way. Yet this does not at all entitle us to hold baptism in contempt. It is not that Christ is bound to baptism as a means of grace, but we in our faith are."[12] It is illegitimate to deduce from the example of the thief on the cross that baptism has no role to play in the appropriation of salvation. If it is possible that children dying in in-

---

[10]A colleague informs me that he was taught as a child that Jesus may have spat at him!

[11]Even if the Longer Ending of Mark is deemed uncanonical, it remains an important witness to the theology of the apostolic age.

[12]*Report of Theological Conversations Sponsored by the World Alliance of Reformed Churches and the Baptist World Alliance, 1977*, "Mission, Church and Baptism," §5, in Harding Meyer and Lukas Vischer, *Growth in Agreement* (New York: Paulist Press, 1984), p. 141. Also online at <www.warc.ch/dt/erl1/03.html>.

fancy can be saved,[13] then they are saved without faith; but that does not mean that faith is an optional extra for adults or that it has no role to play in the appropriation of salvation.

THE AGE OF BAPTISM

An issue not discussed by Bruce Ware is the age of baptism. On this issue Baptists are pulled in two directions, between true "believers' baptism" and "adult baptism." A minority of Baptists are prepared to baptize believers of whatever age. Southern Baptists in the U.S.A. regularly baptize children of seven years old and even younger.[14] This is pure "believers' baptism" since the only condition for baptism is faith and believing children are not excluded on the grounds of their age. The problem with this policy is that few small children reject the views of their parents. In practice it can end up being not too different from the paedobaptist position in that it is effectively the parents who decide when the child is baptized.

Most Baptists opt not for "pure believers' baptism" but rather "mature" or "adult believers' baptism" by setting an age requirement. This is rarely stated explicitly, but most Baptists would not baptize a child under eleven years old and would prefer a significantly older age. Others would look for a maturity more akin to modern adulthood and would prefer not to baptize children before they have been through their years of teenage rebellion.

THE EARLY CHURCH

Bruce Ware claims that, "despite some popular opinion to the contrary, a growing body of scholarship is demonstrating that believers' baptism was the belief and practice of the church for the first four centuries" (p. 47). What exactly is he claiming? If he is arguing that during the first four centuries people were baptized as believers, no

---

[13]In this context, I note that Bruce Ware is unhappy with the idea that "God can regenerate 'a child from the earliest age'" (p. 25), although the experience of John the Baptist (Lk 1:15, 41) would seem to confirm it.

[14]Wayne Grudem, *Systematic Theology: An Introduction to Biblical Doctrine* (Grand Rapids: Zondervan, 1994), p. 982 n. 28, defends this approach.

one would question this. Indeed, given the rapid growth of the church at that time, it is hardly controversial to claim with Stander and Louw[15] that "in the *majority* of instances, it was persons of responsible age (generally adults and grown children) who were the recipients of baptism" and with David Wright[16] that the baptismal experience in the early church "was *largely* of believer's baptism, or perhaps better conversion baptism" (p. 49, my emphases). These quotations that he uses simply confirm my case that while the majority of baptisms may have been such, not all were and that wherever we have clear evidence dual practice is what we find. His own comments, at the beginning and end of this section, appear to claim much more. "Believers' baptism was the belief and practice of the church for the first four centuries" (p. 47). "The conclusions of recent scholarship are that believers' baptism was the conviction and practice for the first four to six centuries of the church as it was of the New Testament church itself" (p. 49). These comments seem to imply that the church of the early Fathers held exclusively to the practice of believers' baptism, without also practicing infant baptism. We have absolutely no evidence that this exclusive practice was *ever* the case. Wherever in the first four centuries there is clear evidence, the picture that emerges is one of dual practice.

[15]Hendrick Stander and Johannes Louw, *Baptism in the Early Church*, rev. ed. (Webster N.Y.: Cary Publications, 2005), p. 119.

[16]David F. Wright, "Recovering Baptism for a New Age of Mission," in *Doing Theology for the People of God: Studies in Honor of J. I. Packer,* ed. Donald Lewis and Alister McGrath (Downers Grove, Ill.: InterVarsity Press, 1996), p. 57.

CONCLUDING RESPONSE

Bruce A. Ware

I AM GRATEFUL FOR THE OPPORTUNITY HERE to reply briefly to the able responses from Professors Ferguson and Lane. In so doing I propose to address some of the key historical, biblical, theological and practical issues raised by one or both of my fellow contributors.

HISTORICAL ARGUMENTS

First, the historical arguments made for their respective positions seem problematic. Professor Lane, of course, places major emphasis on what he sees as the diversity of the practice of baptism in the early centuries of the church. Professor Ferguson, rather, sees many telling indications of paedobaptism in these same early centuries. Since as evangelicals we are committed finally and ultimately to biblical authority, we all recognize that whatever conclusions can be drawn from the practice of the church in its earliest centuries, while instructive and important, can only rightly be viewed as secondary and under both the critique and correction of Scripture itself.

I fear that this observation is most apt in relation to Dr. Lane's proposal which seems to pass over the evidence of the Scriptures—evidence which he gladly acknowledges supports believers' or at least what he calls converts' baptism—to place great stress on the historical record as the primary basis in support of his lenient and nondogmatic position. I fear that Dr. Ferguson's appeal to this early history involves the kind of special pleading against which some more recent studies of this tradition have warned.

More important, we cannot overlook the fact that the most recent and thorough historical studies on the question of baptismal practice in the early church have come to conclusions most strongly favoring the believers' baptism position. I would encourage interested readers to consider the evidence and argumentation presented in the fine historical study by South African Professors Hendrick Stander and Johannes Louw.[1] Appeals to early church theology and/or practice on any given issue are no guarantee that one is directed rightly in accord with the teaching of Scripture. Yet this history is obviously significant, coming as it does on the heels of the New Testament church itself. The fact that the strongest evidence is for a consistent though not absolute practice of believers' baptism provides strong confirmatory evidence for credobaptism. Further, the fact that the spread of infant baptism, understood increasingly as regenerative in its effect, seems to have grown in proportion to the rising fear over the destiny of so many little ones who died in their infancy provides important explanation for the gradual but eventual predominance of infant baptism. In the earlier centuries it was not so, and here the evidence seems most clearly to favor believers' baptism.

BIBLICAL EVIDENCE

Second, biblically I have noted that neither Professor Ferguson nor Professor Lane provided an account for the multiple references in the New Testament that demonstrate a consistent and unbroken pattern (i.e., unbroken by any clear and decisive evidence to the contrary) of baptism being linked with belief in Christ for salvation. Indeed Professor Lane clearly notes this connection but then seems to move away from its implications in favor of what he sees as the historical outworking of acceptable differences on the question of baptism.

---

[1]Hendrick Stander and Johannes Louw, *Baptism in the Early Church*, rev. ed. (Webster N.Y.: Cary Publications, 2005).

Both Drs. Lane and Ferguson appeal to the fact that the New Testament records conversions of adults and hence would naturally make reference to believers' baptism. Their argument fails to take into account the natural fact that the first Christians of the church undoubtedly had many, many infants! Still we find no instruction for parents explaining the new covenant adoption of infant baptism to replace the old covenant's sign of circumcision. This absence is simply incredible if in fact the apostles understood paedobaptism to be the rightful practice in regard to the children of believers. This seems to me something like the elephant in the room. So much evidence in the New Testament points toward the practice of believers' baptism, and no evidence can be given which presents clear and indisputable support to the contrary.

Furthermore, Dr. Ferguson suggests that Peter's inclusion of the phrase "and your children" in his appeal recorded in Acts 2:39 shows the continuity Peter must have had in mind with the children of old covenant believers. Surely the opposite is the case. Peter, speaking to unbelievers, is telling them how to be saved and then receive the promised Holy Spirit, the Spirit who had descended on the church gathered just hours earlier. He tells them if they repent and are baptized they will receive the (promised) Holy Spirit. Then he continues, this promise is for them, for their children, and for as many as are far off, all whom God will call to himself. Far from the reference to children connecting to infant baptism, it connects to children who, when they likewise repent, believe and are baptized, will also receive the promised Holy Spirit. Indeed it seems Peter was in fact a credobaptist, in that he saw the coming of the Spirit as tied to baptism, something which simply cannot rightly apply to paedobaptism.

THE NEW COVENANT AND BAPTISM

Third, theologically it seems clear that the main sticking point and place of contention is over the nature of the new covenant and its relation to baptism. I appreciate Professor Lane's comment that the Lord's Supper is specifically tied to the new covenant. In this he surely is correct. But since the heart of the new covenant is the internalization of the law (Jer 31:31-34) through the indwelling presence and subsequent work of the Holy Spirit (Ezek 36:22-32), it seems right and needful to understand baptism also as tied to the new covenant as the sign that one's old life has now been brought to an end and new life in Christ has been granted, through faith in Christ and by the regenerative and indwelling work of the Spirit.

Further, Professor Ferguson notes with astonishment my affirmation of J. I. Packer's definition of baptism, claiming that credobaptists cannot truly and rightly affirm that baptism is a sign of cleansing and new life in Christ. He argues that Baptists see baptism as a sign of the subjective reality of the faith of the individual but not of the objective work of Christ through which such forgiveness and new life come. Of course Baptists understand baptism as a sign of both the objective and the subjective aspects, not merely of the subjective faith of the believer alone. A professing believer's faith that is conceived as standing apart from the truthfulness and reality of the objective work of Christ upon which genuine faith rests is a shell, a veneer with a hollow core, if seen only in its subjectivity and apart from the objective reality.

Yes, baptism is a sign of faith, but it is in addition a sign of what that faith is trusting in! For Baptists, then, the objective and the subjective are combined, whereas for paedobaptists, in the baptism of infants, the objective is acknowledged by those witnessing the baptism while the subjective affirmation and embrace, which alone gives living expression to what Christ has truly accomplished, is absent altogether. Here then is a real hollowness, but a hollowness in the opposite direction from what Ferguson had pointed. Paedobaptism affirms the reality of Christ's work, in principle, but sees no application or experience of it in the life of the one baptized. For Baptists, the reality (objective) is linked with experience (subjective), and only the combination does justice to that of which baptism truly is a sign—forgiveness of sins and new life in Christ that is real and has really been received by faith!

PRACTICAL APPLICATION

Finally, on issues of practical application, I have already labored the point that Professor Lane's proposal simply is unworkable, even if some might consider it desirable, since it requires all parties to take nondogmatic stances on the issue, accepting that no normative biblical teaching on baptism can rightly be understood from the biblical text. For those of us who believe otherwise, adopting Dr. Lane's position would involve a violation of conscience. It simply is disingenuous, even injurious, to call the church in this direction.

A reply to Dr. Ferguson is needed. In his review of my chapter he comments that I seem to allow no special place for the children of believers within a Baptist theology. If they are not baptized and recognized as children of the covenant, just how are they viewed? Permit me two concluding comments on this question. First, children of Baptist believers are privileged and endued with grace in that they are, in principle, raised in homes and churches where the Bible is taught, the gospel is proclaimed, and instruction and admonishment are given. These activities provide great advantage to the children in their coming to faith in Christ. As Dr. Ferguson acknowledges, children of Bible-believing Baptists and children of Bible-believing Presbyterians are likely raised very similarly. In the best cases, anyway, parents and church leaders undertake the instruction of the young with an earnestness and longing that they grow to know and love the Savior. Honestly, I do not see here how Baptist children are at any disadvantage over their Presbyterian peers.

Second, I do see how Presbyterian children can face dangers that arise precisely from their infant baptism and supposed entrance thereby into the covenant of grace. How many sons and daughters of Presbyterians (even more of Lutherans, and more yet of Roman Catholics) are raised convinced that they are "Christians"—that is, truly saved people, in right relationship with God—precisely because they look back to their baptism as infants to instruct their consciences and grant them confidence of their salvation? Of course where infant baptism is understood as inherently regenerative, this problem is aggravated enormously.

Even where the baptism of infants has no immediate or necessary saving effect, the conception proposed and language used of "children of the covenant" can easily lead both children and parents—and pastors and elders!—to forget that these baptized children are sinners in need of personal salvation through personal faith in Jesus Christ. Yes, Baptists view their children as privileged and blessed in comparison to children raised in non-Christian homes. Baptists also view their children as sinners and rebels against God by nature, outside of the (new) covenant of grace, such that the gospel is regularly proclaimed and instruction is given precisely for the purpose of calling these little ones to faith in Christ for their salvation.

As we all know, all-too-common Baptist practices of manipulative gospel presentations and quick baptisms of young children for whom no care has been taken to assess their spiritual condition create enormous problems, and of this I will gladly (yet oh so sadly) concur. These practices are not what Baptist theology, rightly understood and practiced, would urge. When one sets aside the abuses of Baptist theology and practice and looks squarely at what ought to be believed and practiced vis-à-vis our children, we see a beautiful juxtaposition of perspectives. Our unsaved children are seen both as special but importantly also as sinners, as those surrounded by grace yet needing grace internally and personally, as greatly privileged and instructed in mind while truly lost and needing the law written on their hearts.

Children raised in paedobaptist surroundings can simply progress in understanding the things of the faith, confident of their right standing with God (even if subconsciously) by virtue of being children of the covenant, baptized in infancy, while not recognizing what Baptist parents can never forget. One must believe on the Lord Jesus Christ to be saved, and no manner of training or community participation can change this fact. In this as with all things may the glory be given to Christ, our only Savior and Lord, who truly has accomplished the reality to which baptism, in faith, corresponds.

2

INFANT BAPTISM VIEW

Sinclair B. Ferguson

"I'M FIRST A CHRISTIAN, NEXT A CATHOLIC, then a Calvinist, fourth a Paedobaptist and finally a Presbyterian. I cannot reverse the order" said John ("Rabbi") Duncan, in one of his many Talmud-like aphorisms.[1] What follows is written with a similar sense of priorities. Paul's statement "Christ did not send me to baptize but to preach the gospel" (1 Cor 1:17)[2] expresses a mindset which prioritized gospel preaching over baptismal administration without thereby minimizing the important role of the latter.[3]

Nevertheless our understanding of the gospel inevitably comes to expression in our theology and practice of baptism. Consequently these do sometimes reflect very different perspectives on how the gospel is understood and proclaimed and on what its implications are for biblical hermeneutics and church and family life. Baptism is, after all, an ordinance *of the gospel*. Its theology and practice can never be

---

[1]William Knight, *Colloquia Peripatetica*, 5th ed. (Edinburgh: David Douglas, 1879), p. 8. The wise and eccentric Duncan (1796-1870) was professor of Hebrew in New College, Edinburgh.

[2]All Scripture quotations unless otherwise indicated are from *The Holy Bible: English Standard Version* (Wheaton, Ill.: Crossway Bibles, 2001).

[3]Five letters in the Pauline corpus contain explicit reference to various facets of baptism (Rom 6:1-11; 1 Cor 1:13-17; Gal 3:27; Eph 4:5; Col 2:11-12). Many scholars detect additional allusions in his letters.

divorced from our understanding of its evangelical matrix.

The discussion of different baptismal theologies labors under the immediate difficulty of the misleading nomenclature of baptist and paedobaptist (or infant baptist). In fact we are all baptists. Furthermore paedobaptists baptize *believers* and their children, including infants (*infantes*, literally those who do not speak).[4] Indeed with the collapse of Christendom we baptize believers today probably more frequently than at any time since the Reformation. This is as it always should have been in the church as God's evangelistic agent in the world. It would have been so were it not for the disastrous combination of belief in baptismal regeneration and the Constantinian church-state settlement which led to indiscriminate infant baptism.

On whatever side of the dividing waters of baptism one stands, difficult and as yet impenetrable historical-theological questions arise. Among them are the following:

- If the apostolic churches practiced infant baptism, why are we not able to trace easily in postapostolic literature an unbroken and unquestioned testimony to it from the time of the apostles to the third century?

- If, however, only believers' baptism was practiced in the New Testament church, how is it that infant baptism arose without apparent record of serious theological protest before Tertullian (ca. A.D. 200)?

- Is it in any case wise for evangelicals to appeal to the baptismal *practice* enshrined in the documents of the postapostolic church if, by and large, they are distinctly uncomfortable with the baptismal *doctrine* of the church fathers?

In what follows we will briefly set the scene by tracing the evidence for infant baptism in the postapostolic church (the historical perspective), thereafter provide a biblical-theological perspective on baptism as a whole (the redemptive-historical perspective), before

---

[4]It might be nearer the mark to speak of covenantal-family-baptists and credobaptists in order to stress that different theological *grounds* for baptism are in view, since every year I baptize numbers of believers on profession of faith.

drawing some conclusions about the baptism of the infants of believers (the ecclesiastical perspective).

Baptism in the Postapostolic Church

The witness of early church history to the practice of baptism is frustratingly patchy. Evidence comes essentially from three extant sources. Moving backward in time through them provides us with a snapshot album of baptismal practice in the first three centuries of the church's existence.

Records of mortality. The death inscriptions of early Christianity breathe a remarkable spirit of hope in a world of pagan hopelessness. Some, dating back to the turn of the third century, chronicle early mortality and provide testimony to the faith—and the sadnesses—of Christians.[5] Numbers of mortally ill children were baptized and thus (in the language of the inscriptions) were "made believers" or "obtained the grace of the glorious font." In some cases baptism preceded death by only a matter of hours. Infants were among those who received "clinical" baptism in this way. These infants and children had not already been baptized. This might seem to be proof negative against the idea that the early church already practiced infant baptism. Professor Everett Ferguson has suggested that these death inscriptions give a substantial hint that widespread infant baptism actually grew out of the practice of clinical baptism. However, this strand of evidence belongs to the period when baptism was already being postponed through fear of the risk of postbaptismal sin. It is doubtful if any concrete, rather than speculative, conclusions can be drawn from it.

---

[5]See the discussions and contrasting conclusions in Joachim Jeremias, *Infant Baptism in the First Four Centuries* (London: SCM Press), 1960; idem, *The Origins of Infant Baptism* (Naperville, Ill.: Allenson, 1963); and Kurt Aland, *Did the Early Church Baptize Infants?* (Philadelphia: Westminster Press, 1963). See also Everett Ferguson, "Inscriptions and the Origin of Infant Baptism," *Journal of Theological Studies,* n.s., 30 (1979): 37-46; idem, *Early Christians Speak* (Abilene, Tex.: Abilene Christian University Press, 1987), pp. 55-65. Unfortunately Professor Ferguson's *Baptism in the Early Church: History, Theology, and Liturgy in the First Five Centuries* (Grand Rapids: Eerdmans, 2009) appeared only as these pages were going to press.

Works of theology. The church's transition to the postponement of baptism stands in marked contrast to apostolic example (e.g., Acts 2:41; 8:34-39; 9:18; 10:48; 16:33), but is detailed in postapostolic teaching. Thus Tertullian (ca. 160/70-215/20), in his *De Baptismo*, argues that baptism should be delayed lest it be received without a serious appreciation of its meaning.[6] This reaction—in his case set within the context of perceived laxity in the church—would eventually drive him into the arms of the Montanist sect. But his arguments indicate that already by his time the practice of infant baptism was widespread, even if they do not by themselves indicate how long that had been the case.

Statements prior to this are consistent with infant baptism and fit well with its practice, but fall short of proof. Into this category fit the well-known words of Polycarp at the time of his martyrdom (155/160) detailing 86 years of Christian life.[7] Irenaeus (fl. 175-195) speaks of infants being "born again" to God, in a context in which "regeneration" and baptism appear to coalesce in his thinking.[8] Certainly Origen (ca. 185-ca. 254) believed that the church had received the tradition of infant baptism from the apostles.[9] In contrast to Tertullian, Cyprian of Carthage (ca. 200/10-258) affirms that baptism should be administered as early in life and as soon as possible.[10]

---

[6]Tertullian argues that both the baptized person and his or her sponsors (in the case of an infant) may lapse and thus be placed in a perilous condition in view of, e.g., Heb 6:4-6: "If any understand the weighty import of baptism, they will fear its reception more than its delay." Hence he affirms, "the delay of baptism is preferable; principally, however, in the case of little children." *On Baptism* 18 (*ANF* 3:678). Cf. also Tertullian *On Repentance* 7 (*ANF* 3:663). His *Against Marcion* 1.28.2 (*ANF* 3:293) contains probably his clearest statement on the effects of baptism.

[7]"For eighty-six years I have been his servant, and he has done me no wrong. How can I blaspheme my King who saved me?" The words are, however, inconclusive with respect to the actual timing of his baptism (*The Martyrdom of Polycarp* 9 [*AF*, p. 139]).

[8]*Against Heresies* 2.22.4. His language elsewhere underlines the intimacy of the connection, cf. 3.17.1.

[9]*Commentary on Roman* 5.9.11 (FC 103, p. 367). "It is on this account as well that the Church has received the tradition from the apostles to give baptism even to little children." The context (Origen has cited Ps 51:5) implies a reference here to *infant* children.

[10]In a letter to Fidus. *The Epistles of Cyprian* 58 (*ANF* 5:353-54).

Prior to this point the extant evidence in, for example, *The Epistles* of Ignatius (ca. 100), *The Epistle of Barnabas* (ca. 70-130) and *The Shepherd* of Hermas (ca. 150) remains silent. No certain answers to the historical questions delineated above are provided.

Evidence from liturgy. The practice of infant baptism is confirmed by the *Apostolic Tradition*.[11] Like similarly named pieces (e.g., The Apostles' Creed), this is *post*apostolic in origin and was probably compiled by Hippolytus of Rome (d. ca. A.D. 236). It details a three-year preparatory class required for new communicants and describes their subsequent baptism. Noteworthy are several elements in the extended liturgy. One is the observation that martyrdom serves as baptism in one's own blood.[12] Others include the extrabiblical practice of the prebaptismal all-night vigil, exorcism, sufflation, the laying on of hands and anointing.[13]

Candidates for baptism were received in a fixed order: first, children, then men and finally women (possibly because all were baptized after the removal of clothing). For our purposes the liturgy for the children is especially interesting: "And first the little children are to be baptized; and if he is able to speak for himself, he is to speak [i.e., make the confession of faith in accordance with the Creed of the church in Rome—an early form of the Apostles' Creed]; and if they are not able, their parents are to speak on their behalf or one of their relatives." The confession was made in connection with the trinitarian structure of the creed, and in that connection triune baptism was administered.[14]

The controversial Hippolytus certainly regarded himself as a conservator. There is no adequate reason to doubt that he is detailing an already well-developed tradition in the church of Rome (and elsewhere) by the end of the second century A.D. Several features are noteworthy:

---

[11]See Paul F. Bradshaw, Maxwell E. Johnson, L. Edward Phillips, *The Apostolic Tradition: A Commentary,* ed. H. W. Attridge, Hermenein (Minneapolis: Fortress, 2002).

[12]Ibid., pp. 102-3.

[13]Ibid., pp. 104-7.

[14]Ibid., pp. 112-17.

- The New Testament's pattern of "immediate" conversions has given way to a pattern of conversion following extensive instruction.

- Baptism itself is viewed not only as the rite of initiation but as the actual point of transition from the old to the new life.[15]

- When "outsiders" were baptized, their children accompanied them and confessed the Christian faith themselves. Young children who were *infantes* were also baptized, but on the basis of a confession made by their parents or others.

This last feature in the liturgy gives further indication that infant baptism was practiced in the Latin church before the end of the second century, and therefore within a century of the death of the apostles. What is less clear, however, is the precise basis on which the infant was baptized. The words "their parents are to speak on their behalf" suggest that they may have given answer to the same questions addressed to older children and adults. In itself this does not fully clarify the theological basis of infant baptism. Was the title to baptism of these children grounded in either (1) the faith of their parents/sponsors?—which would be somewhat akin, as we shall see, to a covenantal approach to infant baptism—or (2) was the confession of the parents/sponsors viewed as an expression of the "faith" of the infants themselves?—which would be in keeping with the wording of later inscriptions describing the deceased infant as being "made a believer" at the point of baptism.

The question itself may well be anachronistic, alien to the mindset of the early church, where the description "believer" did not carry all the psychological connotations it tends to hold for evangelicals today.

The *Didache* (which has been variously dated between the first and the third centuries A.D.) contains only brief, albeit interesting, com-

---

[15]Those who find it difficult to understand how the question "When were you converted?" could ever be legitimately answered *"When I went forward* to be baptized" may find an illuminating analogy in the answer, often-heard in the twentieth century: *"When I went forward* at a Billy Graham Crusade."

ment on baptism, but contains no reference to infants.[16] At this point the historical curtain seems to be drawn, and we are left with silence.

In summary then, evidence for infant baptism exists by the close of the second century. No serious theological explanation of it on the one hand nor apparent protest against it appears until the time of Tertullian.[17] If it were practiced, why this frustrating silence? If it were not, why do we find an equally frustrating absence of recorded protest against such novelty—and that among those who believed false teaching more destructive than martyrdom? These—to say the least, mysterious—facts bring us within living memory of the apostolic period, but still far away from conclusive historical evidence.

Important caveats. In considering the historical evidence it is important to keep in mind the distinction between *good consequence* (i.e., consistent with the evidence but not logically required by the it) and *necessary consequence* (consistent with and logically required by the evidence). The historical evidence, such as it is, can be (indeed, has been!) argued both ways. As it stands, the evidence from the early church is inadequate to ground a logically necessary conclusion either way.

Furthermore, as we have noted, appeal to the authors and liturgies of the first two centuries can be a double-edged sword. Christians familiar with the New Testament often find that a first reading of postapostolic writings presents a staggering contrast to it. It is a commonplace sentiment, albeit sometimes exaggerated, that the gospel of grace was not so clearly grasped by some later Christian leaders as it might have been. Clearly the "traditions"[18] of the apostles were not equally well understood and practiced. Indeed the New Testament itself provides enough evidence to show that almost immediately the apostles had to struggle to maintain unity of doctrine and practice.

---

[16]*Didache* 7-8 (*AF*, p. 259).

[17]That some scholars have interpreted Tertullian as protesting against a long established practice and others against an innovation underlines the principle that arguments from silence are usually reversible.

[18]E.g., 1 Cor 4:17; 2 Thess 2:15; 3:6; 1 Tim 6:2; 2 Tim 1:13-14; 2:2; 3:14.

The baptismal practice and implied theology—certainly as these are described in the extant literature—were soon transformed from the apostolic pattern. Additions of various kinds were made. That was true liturgically (we have no record of the apostles blowing on or anointing new converts, nor prefacing baptism by a three-year catechetical class).

Furthermore baptism and regeneration were seen to coalesce in a manner with which most evangelical theology finds itself distinctly uncomfortable. Thus dogmatic evangelical appeals to the practice in the early church may be somewhat self-defeating if the theology grounding that practice (one "becomes a Christian at baptism") is already regarded as suspect. Evangelical theology has never held the "Catholic" view of the consensus of the early church nor of the authority of historical tradition. Its appeal has consistently been to return to the Scriptures. Without wishing to minimize the importance of the historical or the insights of tradition, we therefore turn now to the exposition of a biblical theology.[19]

BAPTISM AND THE BIBLICAL TESTIMONY

The term *baptism* is universally used of the Christian rite of initiation which employs the element of water and the same basic wording ("I baptize you in the name of the Father and of the Son and of the Holy Spirit").

The meaning of the rite in dispute. The employment of the same words and element (whatever the quantity or mode of application) masks the fact that the church evidences no unanimity about the meaning of the rite itself. Explanations of its significance sometimes differ radically. Without grasping this radical difference in interpretation, isolating the issues involved in the baptismal debate proves

---

[19]Limitations of space make an historical-theological survey of the development of paedobaptism beyond the scope of these pages. Paedobaptists have never spoken with one theological voice. While doubtless a weakness, lack of unity on this point is one characteristic of the fragmentation of Christendom. What follows represents a classical covenantal and Christocentric view of baptism in general and infant baptism in particular.

virtually impossible. To a certain extent participants in the debate talk past one another. The extent to which this is so will emerge in the discussion which follows since in significant ways baptists and paedobaptists differ not only over the subjects (and mode) of baptism but actually over the basic meaning of the sign.

History of divine covenants. Foundational to a biblical theology of baptism is the recognition that baptism's sign character positions it within an ongoing pattern of divine activity. Throughout the history of redemption, God's dealings with his people have always included the use of emblems. His epochal promises were illustrated and confirmed physically and visually as well as verbally.

This pattern appears specifically in the history of divine covenants. To the verbal promise of the *Noahic* covenant[20] was added the physical token of the rainbow in the sky (Gen 9:12-16). The token was a sign of the promise and sealed it, guaranteeing God's faithfulness. The rainbow was in fact first a sign of God's promise to God himself. It then reassured Noah that God himself was reminded to remember his promise! Later the *Abrahamic* covenant had its own sign of circumcision (Gen 17:11), while the "visible" sign of the *Mosaic* covenant was the Sabbath day (Ex 31:16-17).

In their own context each of these covenant signs pointed forward to a fulfillment in the new covenant in Christ. He is the true Noah in whose ark we are saved (1 Pet 3:20-22), the seed of Abraham in whom all the nations of the earth are blessed (Gal 3:13-22), the prophet-leader like Moses in whom the final Exodus took place (Deut 18:15; cf. Lk 9:31, where "spoke of his departure" translates *elegon tēn exodon autou* = i.e., spoke of his exodus).

This background shows that the physical signs of baptism and the Lord's Supper which Jesus instituted belong to a larger pattern and should be interpreted in the light of this biblical-theological tradi-

---

[20]Genesis 6:18: *wahăqimōtî 'et-bĕrîtî 'itāk* ("I will cause-to-stand my covenant with you" rather than the usual "I will cut my covenant") may well imply that a prior covenant bond was already in place. See, e.g., W. J. Dumbrell, *Covenant and Creation* (Exeter, U.K.: Paternoster, 1984), pp. 11-26.

tion. Baptism cannot be fully understood abstracted from this matrix. The Westminster Confession of Faith summarizes well the implications for baptism of this covenantal perspective. Baptism (and all biblical sacraments) are

> holy signs and seals of the covenant of grace, immediately instituted by God, to represent Christ and his benefits; and to confirm our interest in Him: as also, to put a visible difference between those that belong unto the Church and the rest of the world; and solemnly to engage them to the service of God in Christ, according to his Word.[21]

This statement gives expression to an underlying theological logic. Each of these characteristics is specifically mentioned in relation to one or another of God's covenant tokens.

Features of baptism. Since each emblem is analogously related to its particular covenant, it is legitimate to see these features as common to any and all emblems by which God confirms to us his covenant grace. Although these features are not explicitly attributed to baptism, each is evidently true of it:

1. Baptism is a sign and seal of the covenant of grace (a principle so central we will treat it at length below).

2. Baptism was immediately instituted by God (in Christ: Mt 28:19).

3. Baptism represents Christ and confirms to faith the privilege of communion with him (Gal 3:27).

4. Baptism distinguishes its recipients from the world (Rom 6:1-23).

5. Baptism engages those who receive it to serve Christ (Rom 6:3-4).

Points (2) to (5) lie on the surface of the passages of Scripture noted and require little or no discussion, but the overall perspective

---

[21]*The Confession of Faith* 27.1.

they present does. What is involved in saying that baptism is a "sign and seal of the covenant of grace"?

Sign and seal of the covenant of grace. The phrase "sign and seal" is derived from Romans 4:11: "He [Abraham] received the sign of circumcision as a seal of the righteousness that he had by faith while he was still uncircumcised." By what reasoning can this description of circumcision be transferred to baptism? Baptism functions in relationship to the new covenant in Christ in a manner analogous to the function of circumcision in the Abrahamic covenant. In a word, baptism has the same symbolic significance in relationship to fellowship with God as did circumcision.[22]

This is not to say that the two signs are equivalent in every respect. The one signified a promise in embryo given to a man, to his family and to his nation. The other signified the same promise now fulfilled in Christ and extended to people throughout all the nations of the world. The signs belong to different epochs of redemptive history. Thus circumcision by its very nature indicated the restrictions and limitations of the old covenant and the epoch it governed (e.g., it was administered only to male seed). Pentecost—and with it baptism—marked an epochal transition, breaking down gender distinctions peculiar to the old covenant (Acts 2:17-18; Gal 3:26-29) so that the new sign has no gender restriction.

Yet with respect to their distinctive covenants and epochs, both baptism and circumcision share the same core symbolism. Both point to the same promise (Gal 3:13-14) and to the regenerative divine indicative and conversion response imperative arising from that promise both prior to and in the light of its fulfillment in Christ. The fruit of the covenant promise emblematized in circumcision is found in regeneration (Deut 30:6), in cleansing (Is 52:1; Ezek 44:6-7) and in repentance (Deut 10:16; Jer 4:4).[23] Precisely these things are the fruit of Christ's

---

[22]Cf. Paul K. Jewett, *Infant Baptism and the Covenant of Grace* (Grand Rapids: Eerdmans, 1978), p. 88. Jewett's comments on this (disputed) issue merit attention in view of his energetic rejection of infant baptism.

[23]For a still valuable discussion of circumcision, see Patrick Fairbairn, *The Typology of Scripture* (Edinburgh: T & T Clark, 1845-1847), 1:308-15.

work and the inner significance of baptism. It is a symbol of regeneration, cleansing and repentance in Christ (e.g., Acts 2:38; 22:16; Eph 5:26; Col 2:12; Tit 3:5-7; Heb 10:22).

If these are covenant blessings expressed in the rite of circumcision, it follows by parity of reasoning that the sign setting forth and sealing the same blessings in the era of fulfillment must also be a covenant sign. In the words of Jewett, "circumcision means 'essentially' what baptism means in the New Testament."[24]

Expressing this in an abbreviated account of redemptive history, we can say that the inner meaning of circumcision was fulfilled in the covenant curse Christ bore on the cross (Gal 3:13-14). Baptism is the new symbol of this curse-bearing for our sake. Paul expresses this in his densely packed statement in Colossians 2:11-12: "In him also you were circumcised with a circumcision made without hands, by putting off the body of the flesh, by the circumcision of Christ, having been buried with him in baptism, in which you were also raised with him through faith in the powerful working of God, who raised him from the dead."[25]

Circumcision fulfilled in Christ for the nations. Abrahamic circumcision has been fulfilled in "the circumcision of Christ." While there remains debate over whether *tou christou* here is an objective or subjective genitive, the underlying theological driver of the whole section seems to be as follows: Christ entered the Abrahamic line, receiving the covenant symbolism of circumcision (Lk 2:21). In him circumcision found its telos—he was the one who experienced the ultimate reality of the cir-

---

[24]Jewett, *Infant Baptism*, p. 96. It is sometimes claimed that if circumcision replaced baptism the "Council of Jerusalem" (Acts 15) would have solved the issues raised by the "circumcision party" by saying "baptism now replaces circumcision, so the latter is no longer necessary." But such a response would not have clarified the fundamental issue at stake, namely the nature of the gospel.

[25]For a discussion of the complex exegetical issues involved in Col 2:11-13, see Peter T. O'Brien, *Colossians, Philemon,* Word Biblical Commentary 44 (Waco, Tex.: Word, 1982), pp. 114-24. In my own view Paul's focus is on the once-for-all historical work of Christ. In describing it, however, he underlines the cross as the center point of redemptive history by a multilayered use of language which echoes the inner meaning of *both* circumcision and baptism.

cumcision of the cross, being "cut off out of the land of the living" (Is 53:8). His baptism also signified this. John baptized him in water with a view to his real baptism in blood on the cross (cf. Mk 10:38-39; Lk 12:50). In his death and resurrection the core significance of both his circumcision and his baptism, and therefore of Abraham's circumcision and of our baptism, meet.

An epochal shift forward moves from the national element inherent in the administration of the promise given to Abraham to the trans-ethnic international element inherent in the fulfillment of that promise. But the core significance of both rites is Jesus Christ.[26]

Our Lord's institution of baptism is itself set in a specifically cove-nantal context in Matthew 28:18-20, a passage which echoes the history of covenantal redemption.

The telos of the Abrahamic covenant was that in Christ the *nations* would be blessed (Gen 12:1-3). The coming messianic king would receive the *nations* for his inheritance (Ps 2:8), but he would enter his messianic glory through his suffering as the servant of the Lord. He would thereafter "sprinkle many nations; kings shall shut their mouths because of him" (Is 52:15).

When our Lord claims all authority in heaven and earth, he is speaking as the one in whom all covenantal promise has reached its consummation. In this capacity he anticipates the fulfillment of the promises made about the seed of Abraham, the Son of David and the Suffering Servant. In his name the disciples are to disciple and bap-tize the *nations* (Mt 28:19). The baptism inaugurated by the Nations-Blessing-Seed and Servant-King expresses the fulfillment of all God's covenant promises. They are all "Yes!" in him (2 Cor 1:20). To this reality baptism points. Baptism is a sign and seal of the union with Christ and fellowship with the Father given by the Spirit and received by us through faith.

Union with Christ. In baptism, the name of the Lord is given to us

---

[26]Internationalism was, of course, already envisaged in the Abrahamic covenant (Gen 12:1-3).

(Mt 28:18-20). Baptism is a naming ceremony.[27] In this sense baptism into the name of Father, Son and Holy Spirit consummates the triune covenant blessing of the Mosaic epoch (Num 6:22-27). Our great High Priest, Jesus Christ, pronounces the blessing. We are baptized into his name, with a view to his saving resources, his possession, authority and fellowship. Baptism therefore points primarily to Christ, from whom the multifaceted blessings of redemption, justification and sanctification are received by faith-union (1 Cor 1:30).

This teaching appears forcefully in Romans 6:1-23, where Paul speaks of baptism disclosing the blessings of union with Christ in his death to sin, and resurrection to newness of life. He is surely referring here to water baptism. The reality, while not identical to the sign, is identified by and expressed through it. Thus in Galatians 3:27 Paul speaks of baptism as symbolizing the union in which we put on Christ. Similarly in Colossians 2:12 he speaks of being buried in union with Christ in his burial, in baptism.

Paul never loses sight of the fact that baptism is symbol. Otherwise he could not have prioritized gospel preaching over gospel sign as he does in 1 Corinthians 1:14-17 (or shown such apparent amnesia about exactly which members of the Corinthian church he had baptized!). Implicit in this language is that what is symbolized is realized only by the work of the Spirit and consciously enjoyed only through faith.

Fear of an *ex opere operato* theology and the desire to stress the importance of individual faith at this point should not lead us to denude the sign of its rich *objective* significance.[28] What is central to the application of redemption, namely all that is in Christ for his people (Eph 1:3-14), is central to the symbolism and sealing of baptism. The symbolism moves *from the objective to the subjective*. Objective signification grounds the subjective realization. A corresponding imperative has its roots in

---

[27]Cf. E. P. Clowney, *The Church,* Contours of Christian Theology (Downers Grove, Ill.: InterVarsity Press, 1995), p. 278.

[28]In this sense Augustine's notion that baptism is an outward, temporal and visible sign of an inward grace is overly subjectively oriented toward the application of redemption potentially abstracted from its center in the person of Christ. See, e.g., Augustine *On the Catechizing of the Uninstructed* 26.50 (*NPNF*[1] 3:312).

these indicatives of grace. Baptism signifies all that is in Christ for us; it points us to all that he will do in us and all that we are to become in him. These are complementary, not contradictory.

The baptism of Christ. In this sense, our baptism takes its meaning from the inner significance of our Lord's own baptism in which he was identified as both sacrificial victim and sacrificing priest. In our Lord's baptism (Mt 3:13-17 and parallels) he is set forward as the Suffering Servant of God/Lamb of God who takes away the sins of the world (Jn 1:29-36; cf. Is 41:9; 53:7). In the midst of all the baptisms John performs, Christ's is the real baptism: "but for this purpose I came baptizing with water, that he might be revealed to Israel" (Jn 1:31). His baptism identifies him as the one who "will baptize you with the Holy Spirit and fire" (Mt 3:11) because he himself is baptized with the Holy Spirit (in the Jordan) and with fire (in the blood of Calvary). Having received this double baptism (sign and thing signified), he became the Baptizer with the Holy Spirit, uniting his people to himself and cleansing them from sin through that ultimate baptism with which he was to be baptized (Lk 12:50).

In his baptism our Lord is identified as the true Priest who deals with sins. John, who baptizes him, himself stands in the line of the levitical priesthood (Lk 1:5). By his baptism of Jesus (then thirty years old, the stipulated age for undertaking of priestly duties, cf. Num 4:3 with Lk 3:23) and consecration of him with water (see Ex 30:17-21; Lev 8:6), John names him as both Royal Priest and Sacrifice. This one will be baptized with a baptism not of water but of blood, for the sake of his people; he will himself baptize with the Spirit and fire (a prophecy fulfilled both in symbol and reality on the day of Pentecost, Acts 2:1-4). Baptism then points to Jesus Christ, baptized and baptizer. It symbolizes the specific identity in which he provided the rich spiritual resources of salvation.

Fellowship with God the Trinity. Even this glorious reality needs to be set within a broader frame of reference. Christian baptism is trinitarian. It signifies and seals communion with God the Trinity. Perhaps this is the most commonly neglected aspect of both the theology and the implications of baptism. We are to be baptized "in the name [singular] of the Father and of the Son and of the Holy Spirit" (Mt 28:19). The rite therefore proclaims that "our fellowship is with the Father and with his Son, Jesus Christ" (1 Jn 1:3), through the Spirit (1 Jn 5:6-12). Baptism, centered on union with Christ, points to access to the Father, through the blood of the Son and in the energy of the Spirit (Eph 2:18). Baptism therefore points to a salvation that is trinitarian in its deepest roots.[29] Consequently baptism's message is as deep and broad as the trinitarian faith of the gospel itself (Mt 28:18-20). It is the rubric under which we live our whole Christian life.

How does baptism function as a sign and seal? Baptism is a sign in that it pictures—as a "visible word" (Augustine)—the gospel and its blessings. It functions not as a merely representative sign pointing to something absent and distant, but as an exhibitive, even a communicative sign. To use the language of the Reformers, it is not a bare sign (*signum nudum*) but points to and communicates to faith the presence of Christ who is brought into focus in terms of the specific blessings expressed by the sign. By means of the sign the Spirit communicates to faith the blessings in Christ whom the visible sign portrays—just as in the power of the Spirit the Christ who is described in the word-signs of preaching may be communicated to us and received by faith.

To be baptized is to be baptized into Christ's death (Rom 6:1-4). This is the inner meaning of the sign. That meaning is realized in us only by the work of the Spirit and only recognized by us in faith. A dynamic relationship between external action and reality is envisaged. Paul expresses the same principle in relationship to the Lord's Supper: the bread we break and the cup we drink are participation, communion *(koinōnia)*, with the body and blood of Christ (1 Cor 10:16). Similarly the sign of baptism engages faith with the reality it signifies—with the One it signifies!

This explanation does not mean that the sign *contains* what it signi-

---

[29]The repeated statements in Acts 2:38; 10:48; 19:5 that baptism was "in the name of Jesus" should be understood either as Lukan shorthand or perhaps as a deliberate contrast with the baptism of John.

fies any more than the word that is preached *contains* Christ. Rather both are means by which the Spirit can and does communicate to receptive faith the divine blessings the signs signify. Obversely, when met with stubborn unbelief, these signs will confirm the judgment they imply (cf. 1 Cor 11:27-32; cf. Heb 3:7-8; 4:7). This is the signs' covenantal role which we must further explore.

In this sense Augustine's descriptive notion that sacraments are "visible words" is helpful.[30] Just as Christ "communicates" himself to his people through the audible "signs" of the word of God, so he communicates himself through the "visual" sign of baptism.

A seal is a confirmation, or attestation, of that which it seals. The Corinthians were the seal of Paul's apostleship (1 Cor 9:2)—their very existence as a Christian church authenticated his ministry. Here the vital theological question is: *What does baptism seal?* We may express the *status quaestionis* more pointedly: Is baptism primarily a seal *of* faith (i.e., of our response to the gospel) or a seal *to* faith (i.e., of the gospel which elicits our response)?

Romans 4:11 insists that the sign of circumcision was "a seal of the righteousness that he [Abraham] had by faith while he was still uncircumcised." The wording here is significant. Circumcision was not a seal of Abraham's faith response, but of the (covenant) righteousness which he received through faith.

Genesis 17:11 confirms this perspective by noting that circumcision also signified an objective reality, not the faith which responded to that reality. "You shall be circumcised in the flesh of your foreskins, and it shall be a sign of the covenant between me and you." Since the "sign and seal" have reference to the same reality according to Romans 4:11-12, circumcision should also be understood as a seal of the promise of God's grace to be received by faith, not of the faith that received the promise of grace.

Baptism then, by parity of reasoning, is a seal as well as sign of the covenant grace of God in Christ. Sometimes this idea causes diffi-

---

[30]*Tractates on the Gospel of John* 50.3 (*NPNF*[1] 7:344).

culties for students who rightly observe that Paul speaks of sealing in relationship to the work of the Spirit (2 Cor 1:22; Eph 1:13; 4:30). Although some commentators in fact see here a reference to baptism,[31] a more secure interpretation is that the Spirit himself is the seal. If that is the case, has not circumcision (the seal under the old covenant) been replaced by (fulfilled in) the Spirit himself—not by baptism—in the new covenant?

Such a solution would imply a false antithesis in Paul's thinking. For the work of the Spirit as inward seal does not negate the idea of baptism functioning as external (physical and tangible) seal. Two quite different perspectives are in view here: (1) The Holy Spirit inwardly seals the believer; (2) circumcision and baptism externally seal the word of promise and gospel. There is complementarity, not contradiction.

This emphasis on baptism as an external, physical sign of the objective work of Christ as the fulfillment of the covenant, revealed in the power of the Spirit to be received by faith, stands in contrast with two divergent traditions of baptismal theology.

DIVERGENT TRADITIONS OF BAPTISMAL THEOLOGY

Catholic view. In contrast to the teaching of the medieval Roman Catholic Church, particularly as this came to formal expression at the Council of Trent, reformed theology emphasized that sacraments do not contain within themselves or effect what they symbolize *ex opere operato*.[32]

The Council of Trent Canon 6 maintained:

> If any one saith, that the sacraments of the New Law do not contain the grace which they signify; or, that they do not confer that grace on those who do not place an obstacle thereunto; as though they were merely outward signs of grace or justice received through faith, and certain marks of the Christian profession, whereby believers are distinguished amongst men from unbelievers; let him be anathema. . . .

---

[31]For an extensive discussion and critique see Markus Barth, *Ephesians 1-3*, Anchor Bible (New York: Doubleday, 1974), 34:135-43.

[32]See John Calvin *Institutes of the Christian Religion* 4.14.3.

> If any one says that in the three sacraments, to wit, Baptism, Confirmation, and Order, there is not *imprinted in the soul a character*, that is, a certain spiritual and indelible sign, on account of which it cannot be repeated: let him be anathema.[33]

Trent suggests that the recipient is sealed by baptism which leaves a mark inwardly on the soul. By contrast, as we have seen in following the paradigm of circumcision, it is the covenant of grace (and therefore salvation, justification and forgiveness in Christ) that is sealed in the rite of baptism.

Subjectivist view. The covenantal view presented here contrasts with Protestant subjectivist views of baptism, emphasizing as it does that baptism pictures the gospel and signifies grace. Baptism is not primarily a sign and seal *of* faith, but *to* faith. This distinguishes the redemptive-historical view of baptism from a memorialist view which has its focus on our remembering (i.e., that baptism fundamentally signifies my faith, my conversion, my obedience).

A comparison of the confessions of paedobaptist and credobaptist churches makes this difference clear. The credobaptist London Confession of Faith of 1689 was taken over largely from the (paedobaptist) Westminster Confession of Faith of 1647. The London Confession maintained many of Westminster's emphases, but it abbreviates the latter's statement on covenant and removes altogether both the term and the perspective from its exposition of baptism and the Lord's Supper. This perspective, shared by leading early Baptist theologians in the United States, reappears in developed form in the *Baptist Faith and Message* of the Southern Baptist Convention.[34] Here *baptism is a sign of my faith in Christ*:

> Christian baptism is the immersion of a believer in water in the name of the Father, the Son, and the Holy Spirit. It is an act of obedience *symbolizing the believer's faith* in a crucified, buried, and risen Saviour, the be-

---

[33]*The Canons and Decrees of the Council of Trent*, Session 7, Canons 6, 9 (Philip Schaff, ed., *The Creeds of Christendom*, vol. 2, *The Creeds of the Greek and Latin Churches* [1877; reprint, Grand Rapids: Baker, 1977], pp. 120-21, emphasis mine).
[34]First published in 1925 and revised in 1963, 1998 and 2000.

liever's death to sin, the burial of the old life, and the resurrection to
walk in newness of life in Christ Jesus. It is a *testimony to his faith* in the
final resurrection of the dead. Being a church ordinance, it is prerequisite to the privileges of church membership and to the Lord's Supper.[35]

This highlights for us two different paradigms for baptism. The
credobaptist perspective does not want to divorce baptism from
grace, but it *defines* baptism in terms of a focus on faith. The redemptive-
historical view does not minimize the role of faith but stresses that
what is symbolized in baptism is not faith but the Christ in whom
faith rests.

Scripture expresses a dynamic relationship between divine signs
and faith. They point us to Christ to whom faith responds, not first
to the faith which does the responding. In this sense, baptism is first
and foremost a Christocentric emblem, not a fidecentric one.

HOW DOES BAPTISM SIGNIFY AND SEAL
THE COVENANT OF GRACE?

When we say that baptism is a *covenant* sign and seal, we acknowledge that its significance is determined by how we think of the covenant. Indeed the variety of ways in which covenant and gospel are
construed may go a long way to help explain why the church exer-
cizes such wide diversity in baptismal theology.

What do we mean when we say "covenantal"? In Scripture God's
covenant is his self-giving to his family among humanity. As the means
by which he promises salvation and restoration, the covenant is a life-
and-death kind of bond signified and sealed by physical symbols.[36] This
covenant involves two parties, but it is neither a contract drawn up by
nor an agreement reached between two parties. It is sovereignly and
unilaterally disposed. God establishes his covenant with his people. His
people receive it, but they do not contribute to its construction. God's

---

[35]*Baptist Faith and Message,* 2000 edition, paragraph 7. Emphasis mine.
[36]See O. P. Robertson, *The Christ of the Covenants* (Phillipsburg, N.J.: Presbyterian and
Reformed, 1980), pp. 3-15.

covenant is complete as such, prior to any response to it.[37] In this sense God's covenant is unconditional, but this unconditional covenant operates in a carefully conditioned fashion since its grace carries in its wake obligations for the covenanted party.

In the Mosaic covenant Yahweh presents himself as having kept his covenant as the Lord who would bring his people out of bondage in Egypt (Ex 20:2). The people do not complete the covenant by having "no other gods before" the Lord (Ex 20:3). Rather having no other gods represents one way they are to respond to the already completed covenant—by fulfilling the obligations and implications of this redemptive grace. The basic covenant dynamic is shown in figure 1.

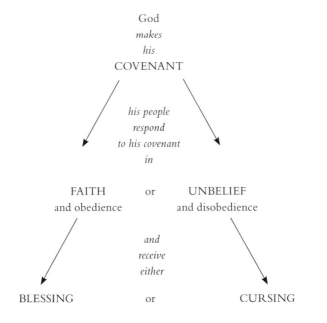

Figure 1. Covenant dynamic

[37]See the seminal work of John Murray, *The Covenant of Grace* (London: Tyndale House, 1954), pp. 10-12.

The redemptive covenants of Scripture all have this structure. Given to people already under the curse, they offer the blessing of salvation to those who trust and obey. If the people spurn the covenant in unbelief and disobedience, the curse remains. This is the pattern with Noah (Gen 5:29; 6:13; 8:21), with Abraham (Gen 15:7-21) and also with Moses (Ex 6:2-8; 34:10-28; Deut 28—30). The pattern finds its ultimate fulfillment in Christ. He enters into humanity's *accursed* situation and bears the divine anathema so that the *blessing* promised to Abraham might come to the Gentiles (Gal 3:13-14; cf. the cry of dereliction Mk 15:34).[38]

Baptism is now the inaugural symbol of what God does in this new covenant in Christ, in which those who are united to the covenant curse-bearing Savior enter into every spiritual blessing in union to Christ (Eph 1:3-14).

Interestingly the two "baptisms" in the Old Testament to which the New Testament makes reference are both water ordeals related to God's forging of a "new" covenant relationship through Noah (i.e., the flood, 1 Pet 3:20-21) and Moses (i.e., the passage through the Red Sea, 1 Cor 10:14). Like Noah and Moses, Jesus Christ had a baptism (water ordeal) to be baptized with to forge his covenant between God and man (Lk 12:50).

In this context, the New Testament's exposition of the passion of Christ draws frequently on Psalm 69,[39] which also describes an ordeal in water.[40] Here Christ is seen to speak (Ps 69:9), and the psalmist's words are interpreted in the light of his passion on our behalf: "Save me, O God! / For the waters have come up to my neck. / I sink in deep mire, / where there is no foothold" (Ps 69:1-2). Christ,

---

[38]The Gospel narrative of the passion of Christ is punctuated by echoes of his covenantal curse-bearing.

[39]Quotations are found in Jn 15:25 (Ps 69:4); Jn 2:17; Rom 15:3 (Ps 69:9); Mt 27:34, 48; Mk 15:23, 36; Lk 23:36; Jn 19:29 (Ps 69:21); Rom 11:9-10 (Ps 69:22-23); Acts 1:20 (Ps 69:25); Phil 4:3; Rev 3:5; 13:8; 17:8; 20:12; 20:15; 21:27 (Ps 69:28). Only Pss 22 and 110 are more frequently cited in the New Testament.

[40]See M. G. Kline, *By Oath Consigned* (Grand Rapids: Eerdmans, 1968), pp. 55-62, especially pp. 59-60.

then, bore the covenant curse (his baptism was realized through the ordeal of the cross) that we might receive the covenant blessing.

In this sense our baptism takes its significance from his baptism into divine judgment, his water ordeal. The reality of his baptism—actual death to and for sin, real judgment curse—means that baptism is no longer an ordeal. When its inner meaning—Christ crucified for us—is grasped, it unfolds for us the cleansing and acceptance with God which we need and which faith receives.

Yet Hebrews underlines that the dynamic enshrined in the old covenant continues to function in the new. For if Christ, the substance of the covenant, is rejected in unbelief and spurned in disobedience, the curse inevitably follows:

> If we deliberately keep on sinning after we have received the knowledge of the truth, no sacrifice for sins is left, but only a fearful expectation of judgment and of raging fire that will consume the enemies of God. Anyone who rejected the law of Moses died without mercy on the testimony of two or three witnesses. How much more severely do you think a man deserves to be punished who has trampled the Son of God under foot, who has treated as an unholy thing the blood of the covenant that sanctified him, and who has insulted the Spirit of grace? (Heb. 10:26-29 NIV)[41]

To this deeply covenantal dynamic inherent in the gospel, God has appended the sign and seal of baptism. It calls us to faith, repentance and blessing. Reject the grace (and the Christ) it signifies, and we remain under the divine curse. Baptism is therefore not efficacious in an *ex opere operato* fashion. Yet it is not a "bare" sign, for it communicates to faith or to unbelief what it symbolizes—covenant blessings to covenant faith, covenant curses to covenant disobedience. "The promise no less threatens wrath to unbelievers than offers grace to believers."[42] What is said about the Lord's Supper also

---

[41]Note that precisely in the context of expounding the fulfillment of the new covenant promise of Jer 31:31-34 (Heb 10:15-18; cf. Heb 8:8-13) the author of Hebrews underlines that the new covenant also knows of an apostasy from it (Heb 10:26-31).

[42]Calvin *Institutes of the Christian Religion* 4.14.14.

expresses mutatis mutandis the covenantal dynamic of baptism: it is possible to receive the sign in judgment rather than in blessing (1 Cor 11:29).

The "proper work" of sacraments, however, is to display Christ as Savior and in the power of the Spirit to fulfill in us all that is treasured up for us in him. As Robert Bruce expressed it, we do not get a better Christ in the sacraments than we do in the Word, but we do often get Christ better; we get a stronger grasp on him through faith.[43] Baptism does not justify, but it is necessary for the believer because he or she remains weak and needs the vivid portrayal of grace which baptism provides.

For paedobaptist believers, the baptism of their children (including infants) is the jewel displayed upon the engagement ring of God's covenant promise. It is of lifelong significance. To this we now turn.

BAPTISM AND INFANTS

The unity of the covenants. Baptism signifies and seals the work of Christ, crucified and resurrected, and the communion with God which is ours through faith.[44] Thus in the New Testament those who came to faith in Christ were baptized (e.g., Acts 2:41; 8:38; 9:18). The organic unity of the covenants of God and of the way of salvation in the old and new covenant epochs inevitably raises the question: Is there such continuity in the administration of God's covenant that children and infants as well as their believing parents continue to receive the inaugural sign and seal of the covenant of grace? Several considerations undergird a positive answer.

The church is organically one throughout the history of redemp-

---

[43]Robert Bruce, *The Mystery of the Lord's Supper,* anglicized and edited by T. F. Torrance (Edinburgh: James Clarke, 1958), p. 64.

[44]It may be worth noting here that the *mode* of baptism has no logical bearing on the issue of its *subjects.* It is sometimes implied that the arguments *for* immersion provide a proof *against* infant baptism. This is poor logic and myopic history. Some Christian groups baptize professing believers by either affusion or aspersion, while others (as diverse theologically as Greek Orthodox and members of the Darby party among the Christian Brethren!) baptize infants by full immersion. No argument for the *subjects* of baptism can be based on its *mode* of baptism.

tive revelation. It consists of those who are embraced by God's covenant. The grace of God is one; the foundation of salvation is one, differently administered in the ages of promise and fulfillment; the instrument of justification is one, namely saving faith; there is one Israel of God.[45] Hence the majority of New Testament illustrations of life in the new covenant are drawn from life in the old covenant, underlining the single redemptive-historical and soteriological underpinning of both epochs of God's grace.

The covenant principle: to you and your seed. Given this organic oneness of the church and the unity-within-progress of the way of salvation (not to mention the expansion of grace implied), the further question arises: Does the pattern of covenantal administration in the old (the principle "to you and your seed") continue through the quantum leap into the new covenant in Christ?

The covenant principle "to you and your seed/children" emerges in the covenant with Noah. Implicit in Genesis 6:18, it is explicit in Genesis 9:9-10: "Behold, I establish my covenant with you and your offspring after you, and with every living creature that is with you, the birds, the livestock, and every beast of the earth with you, as many as came out of the ark; it is for every beast of the earth."

The covenant with Abraham shares this characteristic (Gen 15:18; notice especially Gen 17:1-14). Genesis 17:7-8 summarizes the covenant with Abraham: "And I will establish my covenant between me and you and your offspring after you throughout their generations for an everlasting covenant, to be God to you and to your offspring after you. And I will give to you and to your offspring after you the land of your sojournings, all the land of Canaan, for an everlasting possession, and I will be their God."

The same is true of the covenant with Moses, in which God remembers his covenant with Abraham, Isaac and Jacob (Ex 2:24; cf.

---

[45]Gal 6:16. Cf. the principle of Rom 11:17: the use of epithets describing the new covenant community drawn from descriptions of the old covenant community, and the fact that Christ and the gospel are seen as the divine fulfillment of the covenant already in place (e.g., Lk 1:54, 72).

Ex 6:1-8). That covenant God fulfilled for the Israelite generation contemporary with Moses and for their families (cf. Deut 29:9-14). The same is also true of the covenant with David (Ps 89:3-4, 18-37; cf. 2 Sam 22:51; 23:5).

From the retrospective point of view from Pentecost (the day of covenant transition), divine covenants in redemptive history were made with believers and with their seed—without exception.[46] In one sense "and their seed" was part of the definition of what was involved in a covenant.

Three considerations should be noted here:

1. Covenant administration underlines God's desire and purpose in redemption, namely to restore that which was lost at the Fall. This purpose focuses not merely on individual salvation, but on human beings set in the context of the family. Sin disrupted the relation to God of man-in-family (Gen 3—4). Grace has the design of restoring all the dimensions of this relationship. The covenant administration of grace has therefore a specifically family orientation.

   This underlines the principle that in Scripture the grace of God—that is the gracious God—does not destroy nature but heals *fallen* nature, restoring relationships in antithesis to the destructive work of sin.[47] The manner in which the covenant is administered throughout the Old Testament underlines this. Where this is not recognized, the (unbiblical) notion that grace is antithetical to nature as such creates an inherent suspicion of infant baptism, and leads to a downplaying of the significance of family covenant administration.

2. Since, as we have seen, all former covenant administration includes the children of the covenanted party, and both the people

---

[46]If the Adamic relationship and administration in Eden is regarded as covenantal (e.g., in the Westminster Confession of Faith), it follows from Romans 5:12-21 that the principle "to you and your seed" characterized it also.

[47]Cf. Herman Bavinck, *Our Reasonable Faith* (Grand Rapids: Eerdmans, 1956), p. 277: "Grace is something other and higher than nature, but it nevertheless joins up with nature, does not destroy it but restores it rather."

of God and the way of grace are organically one throughout Scripture, the abrogation of the "you and your seed" principle would require a decisive and specific announcement. Indeed, in the light of the integral relationship between covenant and the seed principle, it may be asked whether it *could* be abandoned and covenantal administration itself remain.

3. On the day of Pentecost Peter specifically emphasized the principle that the covenant promise is still for believers and their seed, just as it was in the Old Testament epochs. Peter announces the epochal advance of God's purposes prophesied by Joel in connection with the last days when the Spirit would be poured out (Joel 2:28-32; Acts 2:17-21): (1) In terms of ethnicity, he will now come on all flesh, including those who are "far off" (Acts 2:39, i.e., Gentiles, Eph 2:17-22). (2) In terms of gender, now both sons and daughters will prophesy (Acts 2:17).

   Yet the underlying principle of administration to believers and their children continues: "The promise is for you and your children" (Acts 2:39) *as well as* for those who are "far off." The promise here is *covenant* promise which has found its fulfillment and substance in Christ himself and in the gift of the Spirit, as Joel had prophesied. It affirmed rather than repudiated the principle of administration characteristic of the old, namely "to you and your children."

   Do not Peter's further words—"everyone whom the Lord our God calls to himself"—abolish this old covenant principle? Stephen Marshall answered that question adequately centuries ago: "except in relation to the Covenant, there was no occasion to name their children, it had been sufficient to have said, a promise is made to as many as the Lord shall call."[48] Peter's inclusion of a category *between* "you" and "all who are far off" underlines the continuity of covenant administration even in the context of its dramatic development. Expansion, not contraction, is in view.

---

[48]Stephen Marshall (ca. 1594-1655), *A Sermon of the Baptizing of Infants* (London, 1644), p. 17.

Summary. The continuity of administration of the covenant signs and the case for the baptizing of the infant seed of believers is thus based on the following considerations:

- All divine covenants prior to the day of Pentecost were made with believers and their seed, so that the community of the people of God always included both believers and their seed.

- The unity of substance of the promise of the covenant and the way of salvation (the promise which circumcision signified) implies that circumcision's replacement[49] can appropriately be given to infants. Otherwise infant circumcision would have been as inappropriate in the old covenant as it is argued infant baptism is in the new.[50]

- The gospel is the new covenant in Christ. Its first proclamation on Pentecost by Peter specifically underscores the continuation of the inner covenant principle that the promise fulfilled in Christ is made to believers and their seed.

- The organic unity of the family is a feature of the whole Bible. The new covenant does not introduce a different view of the family in relation to the administration of God's purpose and its sign, but is in organic continuity with it.

- Baptism is the new sign of the covenant in its fulfillment just as circumcision was the sign of that covenant in the time of promise. Its primary function is not to symbolize our response to the promise of the gospel, but to signify and seal the gospel to which we are called (by the word and the symbol) to respond in lifelong faith and repentance. This is as applicable to infants as it is to others without compromising its significance.

B. B. Warfield pointedly expresses this continuity perspective:

---

[49]See above, Paul Jewett, *Infant Baptism and the Covenant of Grace,* p. 14 n. 2.

[50]The logic and theology of some arguments against infant baptism are, however unwittingly, in danger mutatis mutandis of denying the (divinely ordained!) legitimacy of circumcision.

> The argument in a nutshell is simply this: God established His Church in the days of Abraham and put children into it. They must remain there until he puts them out. He has nowhere put them out. They are still then members of His Church and as such entitled to its ordinances. Among these ordinances is baptism, which standing in similar place in the New Dispensation to circumcision in the Old, is like it to be given to children.[51]

Proponents of believers' baptism at times claim that infant baptism rests on an argument from silence. But both baptists and paedobaptists must make sense of the same silence. It is precisely the silence that demands *theological*, not simply proof-textual, engagement. The paedobaptist conviction is that insofar as the argument is from silence, that silence speaks volumes about the principle of covenant continuity! Insofar as gospel grace remains covenantal, the principle "to you and your children" remains inviolable. The children of believers receive the same promise as their parents and are therefore to be baptized. This, in a nutshell, is the biblical-theological underpinning for infant baptism.

Space constraints forbid any demonstration here of how paedobaptist theology resolves the difficulties thought to attend it. Here it must suffice to indicate some of the ways in which this paradigm coalesces with the broader perspectives of the New Testament.

THE HARMONY OF PAEDOBAPTISM WITH THE NEW TESTAMENT MINDSET

The covenantal paradigm which we have discussed emerges in a variety of ways in the teaching of the New Testament and is written into the warp and woof of its teaching.

The household. The occurrence of household baptisms in the New Testament is best understood as an expression of the Old Testament covenantal principle of the solidarity of the family. Several such baptisms are recorded in the New Testament (Acts 16:15, 33-34; 1 Cor

---

[51]B. B. Warfield, *Studies in Theology* (New York: Oxford University Press, 1932), p. 408.

1:16). Baptism of households appears to have been relatively commonplace in the early church.

While the very idea of a "household" assumes the possibility
(even statistical probability) of a wide variety of age, including children and infants, this per se is not the significant point.[52] The point
is that the baptism of an entire household as such (Acts 16:15; 1 Cor
1:16) echoes the pattern governing circumcision in Genesis 17:11-14.
The New Testament term *oikos* ("household") translates the Hebrew word *bayit*. Throughout the Old Testament it signifies the entire family, even the extended family, and automatically includes all
members whatever their ages. In particular, the Hebrew term expresses the corporate concept of family in the biblical world, in distinction from the atomistic concept of individuality characteristic of
our post-Enlightenment (and postmodern) world.

God's dealings with families. God deals with families (Ps 68:6). Paedobaptism is consistent with this perspective. Its obverse, while ac-
knowledging that God may thus work, must see such working as a
strictly unexpected divine providence rather than a standing divine
principle rooted in covenanted promise. Once pulled, this thread has
a tendency to continue to unravel until the Bible's view of the family
is destroyed. Opposition to the covenantal view implies that in the
new covenant God has radically transformed his principles of operation, has ceased to view families in the same way and sees them now
as atomistic individuals, at best related in his decreed purposes but
not in his expressed promises. By contrast the ongoing employment
in the New Testament of the household concept suggests continuity
not discontinuity.

This continuity is further exhibited in the way in which Paul's
letters include children as "saints" and exhort them to fulfill specifically covenantal responsibilities: "Obey your parents *in the Lord* for
this is right" (Eph 1:1; 6:1-3; cf. Col 1:2; 3:20). Paul's appeal to the
words of the Mosaic covenant in the Ephesians context implies that

---

[52]The relevant texts have been variously interpreted and would require a lengthier ex-
amination than is possible here.

the same covenant dynamic which grounded the relationship of parents and children in the old continues in the new.

Parents and children. These scriptures also provide the model for the view paedobaptist parents are to have of their children and of the nature of their mutual responsibilities. Paul regards the children of believers as children of the covenant. He assumes specifically that the promise of God is given to them. He therefore continues the old covenant pattern[53] in which children were exhorted: "you have been circumcised, therefore live out a life of faith and repentance." But mutatis mutandis, this is how he speaks to new covenant children—in a manner which perfectly expresses the outworking of the principles of new covenant baptism: "Children, you have been baptized; therefore express your faith and repentance in a lifestyle of faithfulness to the Lord in the very first sphere in which he himself was faithful—the home!"

The blessing of infants by Christ. It is not necessary here to adopt the view that the use of the verb *kōluō* (hinder) in this context signals a *Sitz im Leben* in the early church's practice of baptism (cf. Acts 8:36; 10:47). The Gospel pericope of Christ blessing the children (Lk 18:15-17; Mk 10:13-16) further confirms our general approach to the status of children in the covenant community. Paedobaptist liturgies often cite this pericope, which has thus, with some frequency, become a focus for credobaptist criticism.[54]

Some have argued that Luke's version of the pericope, in which Mark's *ta paidia* (children) becomes *ta brephē* (probably babies, infants—the term can be used even of an embryo) suggests that the incident was already being appealed to as a rationale for infant baptism.[55] This may prove to have been a fascinating piece of New

---

[53]Cf. Deut 6:4; Ps 51:6; 119:11, 14, 16, 20, 24, 32, 36.

[54]For example C. H. Spurgeon's sermon, "Children Brought to Christ, Not to the Font," *The Metropolitan Tabernacle Pulpit* (London: Passmore and Alabaster, 1865), 10:581-588.

[55]Joachim Jeremias had already raised the question of a baptismal formula in his article "Les traces d'une Formule Baptismale dans le Nouveau Testament," *Revue d'Histoire et de Philosophie Religieuse* 17 (1937): 424-34. For Oscar Cullmann's exposition see his *Baptism in the New Testament,* trans. J. K. S. Reid, SBT 1 (London, SCM Press, 1950), pp. 76-79.

Testament detective work, but it can hardly commend itself to a paedobaptist Sherlock Holmes or a credobaptist Dr. Watson as "elementary"!

Nevertheless great significance attaches itself to this pericope, notably in the words of our Lord, "to such [infants] belongs the kingdom of God" (Mk 10:14; Lk 18:16). The statement *tōn gar toioutōn estin hē basileia tou theou* ("for of such is the kingdom of God") does not, indeed cannot, mean "the kingdom belongs to those who share the childlike qualities [e.g., dependence, trust, etc.], these infants have, but [of course] not to these particular infants."[56] The correlative adjective *toioutōn* (such) introduces an inclusive category, not a comparison. It signifies "these and such as these," not "those like these, but not these."

The expression "to such as these" cannot therefore exclude these specific infants, but must include them. Of such is the kingdom of heaven. If "of such is the kingdom" (in whatever sense), of such also is the title to the sign of the kingdom, which, according to the King, is baptism (Mt 28:18-20). This is the nub of the paedobaptist use of our Lord's declaration.

The much-feared implication of indiscriminate baby baptism is a diameter removed from this. In fact the passage carefully guards us against it. For "these" infants are precisely ones whose parents[57] bring them to Christ. By deliberate choice they come for the blessing of the Son of God.

Why then, if this is so consistent with the practice of infant baptism, did Jesus not baptize them, but "merely bless them"? Two things should be noted here.

---

[56]The tendency (begun with Origen) to take the words "whoever does not receive the kingdom of God as a child" (Mk 10:15; Lk 18:17) as epexegetical of "to such belongs the kingdom of God" ignores the fact that here *toioutōn* (Mk 10:14; Lk. 18:16) requires the inclusion of these particular children/infants, not their exclusion. It would be pedantic to insist that *erchesthai* (to come) here implies the ability to walk. Being brought by parents *is* how infants "come."

[57]The plural pronoun "them" (*autois*, Lk 18:15) is masculine in form. Fathers were, apparently, present!

Jesus himself baptized no one (Jn 4:2). While his disciples engaged in baptizing within the context of John's ministry (Jn 3:22; 4:1-2), nothing indicates that they continued to do so in the ensuing years of Jesus' ministry. It would seem to have been inappropriate for our Lord to have baptized in connection with his own ministry at this stage in redemptive history, prior to the reality prophesied in his own baptism in the Jordan.

The idea that Jesus "merely blessed" these children ignores the theological depth of nuance in this biblical language and reads the narrative illegitimately abstracted from the flow of the redemptive historical theology of Scripture. This pericope is full of biblical-theological echoes, being reminiscent, for one thing, of the action of God in the Exodus taking up his people and carrying them as a father carries his son (Deut 1:31). Here the one engaged in the true and final exodus (cf. Lk 9:31[58]) emulates his Father. The Great High Priest of the new covenant pronounces his own benediction, "The Lord bless you . . ." (Num 6:24-26).

Of special importance is the linguistic evidence that the language of "bless" and "curse," as we have already noted, is deeply covenantal. The presence of either term signals the operation of God's covenant. Thus the action of Jesus is described in terms of covenant and kingdom blessing. Since "of such is the kingdom of God" and since the covenant Lord pronounces on them the covenant blessing, the theological foundation for infant baptism is already laid. Its actual administration only awaits the new age ushered in through his own blood-and-fire baptism on the cross and his emergence from it in the resurrection and ascension.

THE IMPLICATIONS OF BAPTISM

What, then, are the practical implications and values of infant baptism?[59] The efficacy of baptism is not tied to the moment of its

---

[58]See the discussion above, pp. 96-100.

[59]It is appropriate for both paedobaptist and baptist traditions to confess our shared failure in rightly administering baptism, and often wrongly, if silently, conveying false

administration. One thinks here of Martin Luther encouraging himself throughout his Christian life by saying "*baptizatus sum*" (I am a baptized person). This well reflects the appeal of the New Testament: "Do you not know that all of us who have been baptized into Christ Jesus were baptized into his death? . . . Buried therefore with him by baptism . . . in order that, just as Christ was raised . . . we too might walk in newness of life. . . . Let not sin therefore reign" (Rom 6:3-12). Baptism is the rubric under which the entire liturgy of the Christian life is expressed. The implications of this are summarized in *The Larger Catechism* of the Westminster Assembly.

> *Question:*
> How is our baptism to be improved by us?
> *Answer:*
> The needful, but much neglected duty of improving our baptism, is to be performed by us all our life long, especially in the time of temptation, and when we are present at the administration of it to others; by serious and thankful consideration of the nature of it, and of the ends for which Christ instituted it, the privileges and benefits conferred and sealed thereby, and our solemn vow made therein; by being humbled for our sinful defilement, our falling short of and walking contrary to, the grace of baptism, and our engagements; by growing up to assurance of pardon of sin, and of all other blessings sealed to us in that sacrament; by drawing strength from the death and resurrection of Christ, into whom we were baptized, for the mortifying of sin and the quickening of grace; and by endeavouring to live by faith, to have our conversation in holiness and righteousness, as those that have therein given up their names to Christ; and to walk in brotherly love, as being baptized by the same Spirit into one body.[60]

This extends into the life of the covenant family. Since the sign is ours and also our children's, the principles of Ephesians 6:1-4 apply to every aspect of parental responsibility and children's experience.

None of this should be misunderstood as implying that paedobap-

---

impressions and misleading spiritual hopes in the process.
[60]*The Larger Catechism,* question 167.

tists believe their children do not need to "be converted." True, many children from Christian families cannot remember a decisive "conversion" moment, but "conversion" should not be reduced to a moment of psychological crisis. It is simply shorthand for the faith and repentance which mark the continuance as well as the beginning of the Christian life. The gospel sign of baptism—whether received in infancy or in later years on profession of faith—calls us all to this lifelong conversion.[61]

Father and son, mother and daughter therefore stand together as recipients of the covenant. Their obedience of faith will express itself in different ways, in each case appropriate to their distinctive stages in life and roles within the family—the father loving his wife and not exasperating or embittering his children, lest they be discouraged, but bringing them up in the training and instruction of the Lord; the wife loving her husband and submitting to him in reverence for the covenant Lord as she, with her husband raises their children; the children obeying their parents, in the Lord, because it is right so to do, and because obedience to this covenant command (fascinatingly, the only command in the Decalogue without a single negative overtone!) is especially encouraged by a unique promise of blessing (Eph 6:1-4). Like their Lord, within the context of a covenant family, baptized children are called to grow in wisdom as they grow in stature, and by his grace in favor with God and man (Lk 2:52).

Thus infant baptism, set as it should be within a household of faith and the community life of the church of Christ, will never be regarded as a *signum nudum*. From the very beginning of life the words *"baptizatus sum"* or *"baptizata sum"* (in the case of Latin-speaking daughters!) are relevant to every member of the covenant family. Throughout the whole of our Christian lives our baptism points us to Christ and to all the blessings faith finds in him. It is a perpetual reminder of Christ's grace and a summons to an entire life of trust and obedience.

---

[61]As the first of Luther's Ninety-Five Theses makes plain: "When our Lord Jesus Christ said 'repent!' he meant that the whole of the Christian life should be repentance."

BELIEVERS' BAPTISM RESPONSE

Bruce A. Ware

I AM GRATEFUL FOR THE SUPERB CHAPTER provided by Sinclair Ferguson defending infant baptism. It stands as one of the finest and most able defenses I have read. I believe that it helps demonstrate how some, indeed many, find this view compelling. Alas, I am not among those so compelled. In what follows I shall offer only the responses I believe most important, trusting that the reader will study in addition my own chapter in which I have interacted throughout with various aspects of the paedobaptist position.

First, the historical argument presented by Ferguson seems to me much more optimistic in its support of an early established paedobaptist practice than I believe the historical data warrant. Of course all sides recognize that the paucity of relevant information makes any and all conclusions necessarily tentative. Nevertheless it appears likely from recent historic study that an earlier paedobaptist historiography was overly inclined to find infant baptism where there was none—or at least where none was clearly to be found. As some recent historical studies have pointed out, mention of the baptism of children has sometimes been taken as evidence for the baptism of infants, where this simply cannot be demonstrated. While all sides agree that the historical argument is secondary and that what Scripture teaches is primary, nonetheless, it seems most probable that the picture from early church practice of the first several centuries favors believers' baptism, with infant baptism increasing along with stronger desires to secure the salvation of those who die in infancy.

Second, Ferguson's understanding of baptism as sign and seal at one level can be accepted and applauded by Baptists as exactly right. In answering the question, "What does baptism signify and seal?" he writes, "Baptism is a sign and seal of the union with Christ and fellowship with the Father given by the Spirit and received by us through faith" (p. 89). Amen and amen!

The fact that paedobaptists speak with such clarity about baptism's connection to union with Christ and the indwelling of the Spirit by faith has led more than one reader of the paedobaptist argument to wonder just how infants qualify. By nature, infants cannot yet have believed and so are neither united with Christ nor indwelt with the Spirit. Of course, then, the paedobaptist argument depends on seeing baptism as sign and seal of the new covenant in a fashion parallel to circumcision as sign and seal of the old.

I will not repeat in full here the argument against this understanding I have made in my own chapter. Suffice it to say that this is exactly where the main theological difference between credobaptists and paedobaptists occurs. Whether the move from circumcision as the sign and seal of the covenant with Abraham extends forward with fundamental continuity or with some significant discontinuity to the sign and seal of baptism for the new covenant—here is where the main theological difference is most sharply seen. As I endeavored to explain, the fact that circumcision functioned at two levels, both for the ethnic and national people of Israel and for the spiritual reality of being separated unto God, indicates that the sign and seal of baptism simply is not meant to be seen as parallel to circumcision. Rather than being one nation, the community of the new covenant is composed of believers in Christ from every people, tribe and nation. The function of national identity drops out in the new covenant. In its place is the multiethnic, multinational church of Jesus Christ. As such baptism functions only in relation to the spiritual reality and not in relation to the ethnic and national reality as circumcision previously had.

When Ferguson writes that "with respect to their distinctive covenants and epochs both baptism and circumcision share the same core symbolism" p. 87, it becomes clear that he fails to appreciate fully the role that circumcision played in marking off a particular ethnic and national people as those separated unto Yahweh, chosen as a distinctive people from all other nations and peoples on the face of the earth (Deut 7:6-8). That Israel marked infant males by circumcision as part of this distinctive ethnic and national people of God was crucial to the identity of Israel as the nation she was, and as the people through whom the promised Messiah would come. His coming would bring salvation not only to Israel but through her to the other nations of the world. Precisely because in the new covenant both Jew and Gentile are united in "one new man" (Eph 2:15) where "circumcision is nothing, and uncircumcision is nothing" (1 Cor 7:19 NRSV; cf. Gal 5:6), it simply is wrong to carry forward the function of circumcision as a marker of a distinctive ethnic, national people into the new reality of those, from any and every nation, who are united by faith to Christ.

That is not to deny any relation between circumcision and baptism. Where circumcision and baptism are parallel is exactly where Colossians 2:11-12 see them as parallel, namely, in the spiritual reality to which each of them points. When one ponders the question of the *nature* of the circumcision that *is* parallel to baptism, it is clear that it is spiritual, not physical, circumcision. Paul could not be clearer: "In him also you were circumcised with a circumcision *made without hands* [i.e., *not* physical circumcision], by putting off the body of the flesh, by the circumcision of Christ" (Col 2:11, emphasis added). The nature of this circumcision marks one off as spiritually united with Christ, having died to the flesh and now living to Christ. When Paul continues that those who were circumcised with a circumcision made without hands are those who have been "buried with him in baptism" (Col 2:12), it becomes clear that baptism parallels the spiritual reality to which circumcision pointed and not the physical descent marked by infant circumcision. In short, the parallel between circumcision and baptism in the new covenant is not between physical circumcision and infant baptism; rather, the parallel is between spiritual circumcision of the heart and baptism, which signifies regeneration, faith and union with Christ.

Precisely here the credobaptist is most deeply troubled with the paedobaptist position. If baptism rightly understood signifies the *reality* and not merely the *promise* of union with Christ through faith, then the practice of infant baptism communicates something deeply flawed. Since by nature infants cannot have come to understand or embrace the reality of their own sin, or the gracious redemptive work done in Christ, or the necessity of faith apart from works to receive God's free gift of eternal life—that is, since infants cannot have any of this understanding or experience of regeneration or new life in Christ, they simply cannot be those for whom the reality of union with Christ is true. Baptism, which signifies the reality of such union with Christ, must only be performed—yet it truly must be performed—on those who have personally acknowledged their own sin and confessed personal faith in Christ as Savior and Lord.

This is not to say that union with Christ offers no promise! Indeed it does. The gospel is the promise that all those who trust in Christ alone for the forgiveness of their sin and the hope of eternal life will be saved. As Peter said on the day of Pentecost (Acts 2:39), the promise of forgiveness of sins and the powerful reception of the Holy Spirit is extended now to those listening to Peter's words, and to their children, and to all people throughout all the world (cf. Mt 28:19-20; Acts 1:8). The gospel itself, then, is the promise of new life in Christ. Its good news is to be broadcast throughout the nations and to the ends of the earth.

Baptism, though, does not function first and foremost as a statement or sign of this promise; rather baptism functions first and foremost as a statement or sign of the promise *fulfilled* in the life of one who has personally trusted Christ and has been united with him in his death, burial and resurrection to newness of life. While baptism announces to those watching the immersion of a believer that new life in Christ is available for those who confess Christ as their Savior and Lord, yet baptism itself is directly a sign of this reality having been fulfilled in the life of the one who is himself or herself baptized. Baptism announces in symbolism that is rich and beautiful—that is, baptism by immersion pictures one's union with Christ's death and resurrection in cleansing of sin and newness of life—the reality of sins forgiven and risen life in Christ, the believer's only hope.

So then, since only the actual spiritual *reality* is in view when one is baptized, the sign and seal of baptism relates only to those who have experienced this spiritual reality, that is, to believers in Jesus Christ. The new covenant encompasses only those who know the Lord, those who have been united with Christ, those in whom the Spirit has come to dwell through faith. As such, baptism, the sign and seal of this reality (i.e., not of the promise but of the reality itself), applies rightly only to believers in Jesus Christ.

Third, Ferguson and all paedobaptists must recognize the uniformity of the New Testament teaching on baptism as applied to believers. My purpose in listing so many passages (eleven separate accounts) from the book of Acts is simple: Luke presents a clear and unambiguous depiction of baptism as being performed on believers. The absence both of any clear and convincing example of infant baptism in the New Testament and the absence of any apostolic teaching that baptism had taken the place of circumcision—both of these silences, as it were—are significant and loud, especially when set alongside the abundance of examples of believers' baptism. Clearly the burden of proof is on the paedobaptist to demonstrate that this uniform historical record in Acts should not be seen as the norm for the Christian church.

The weight of this evidence from the book of Acts, then, should be considered in relation to Ferguson's discussion of the meaning of Romans 4:11 as it pertains to what circumcision actually seals and the implication he draws from this for baptism. Two comments are in order.

1. Ferguson argues that Paul has made clear that circumcision is the seal not of the faith-response of Abraham but of the objective reality of the righteousness that God credited to him by faith. Ferguson is correct that circumcision is a seal of the "righteousness" Abraham had received and hence of the objective reality and truth of this as it pertains to his own life. One cannot separate this objective reality from the fact that it was received subjectively "by faith." So Paul's statement in Romans 4:11 combines the objective and subjective features when he writes that circumcision was a seal of the "righteousness of faith" which Abraham had while he was yet uncircumcised. Surely as Paul is making this point about Abraham himself, one cannot say that circumcision functioned exclusively as the objective reality devoid of its subjective appropriation. As the phrase "righteousness by faith" indicates, just the opposite is true. The objective standing of righteousness and the subjective appropriation by faith are viewed together.

2. Still further Paul makes no connection here between Abraham's circumcision and new covenant baptism. It is then a stretch to make this link, as paedobaptists are wont to do, which the text does not here encourage. Rather Paul's point at this juncture in the argument of Romans 4 is a simple one: Abraham was reckoned righteous by faith apart from circumcision, so that he might be the father of those today (Gentiles particularly) who likewise are reckoned righteous by faith and apart from circumcision. As Schreiner comments on Paul's main point in Romans 4:11, Paul is affirming that "one should not interpret the authenticating and confirming role of circumcision in such a way that it is construed to be indispensable for righteousness. The uncircumcised person is at no disadvantage in lacking the sign, because righteousness is available by faith without submitting to circumcision."[1] Clearly nothing in

---

[1]Thomas R. Schreiner, *Romans*, Baker Exegetical Commentary on the New Testament, ed. Moisés Silva (Grand Rapids: Baker, 1998), p. 225.

Paul's teaching in the verse links circumcision to baptism. Hence to apply this teaching to baptism goes beyond the text of Scripture and does so strictly for prior theological interests that are at best brought to the text, not drawn out of the text. Ferguson's use of Romans 4:11 both misses the subjective reality of Abraham's own faith as a necessary condition for his being reckoned righteous and applies this text to baptism in a manner foreign to the meaning of the text itself.

In the end one must consider whether a nuanced theological argument for infant baptism which seems somewhat removed from the text of the New Testament can be sustained against the consistent and plentiful evidence of the book of Acts and the New Testament epistles. These New Testament references show that baptism symbolizes the reality of one's identification with Christ, in his death and resurrection, such that only and always it is believers (no clear exception to this fact appears in the New Testament) who are the subjects of baptism.

The Baptist conviction, then, is one driven by the text of the New Testament. Granted this reading of the text has an accompanying theological understanding which allows for some level of discontinuity between God's dealings with Israel as a national and ethnic people, peculiar among the nations of the world, from God's dealings with the multiethnic and multinational church of the new covenant, composed of Jew and Gentile joined together in one new body in Christ. Just as the author to the Hebrews underscores the importance of the discontinuity between the old and new covenants and at the same time acknowledges legitimate parallels and continuities, so too here the Baptist conviction seeks to read redemptive history rightly, with both its lines of continuity and with its brilliant and spectacular discontinuities. It appears, then, that God has intended baptism to function in some important ways differently than circumcision did under the old covenant. The sign of baptism, it appears from all of the evidence that the New Testament affords us, is designed by God as a sign of the *reality of union with Christ by faith*

experienced in the life of one who has believed in Christ alone for salvation.
If God so designs this distinctiveness to characterize the rite of baptism, may we celebrate the newness of the new covenant along with
the newness and distinctiveness of its glorious new sign.

DUAL-PRACTICE
BAPTISM RESPONSE
Anthony N. S. Lane

SINCLAIR FERGUSON'S ESSAY IS, as one would anticipate, a very able exposition and defense of the Reformed covenant theology approach to infant baptism. Almost I am persuaded—but not quite! If I do not agree with him, it is not because he has stated the case badly but rather because the case itself is (in my view) seriously flawed.

COVENANT OR COVENANTS?

The covenant theology argument for infant baptism relies on the premise that there is only one covenant of grace. Where does Sinclair Ferguson stand on this? He never refers to the "one covenant of grace" in so many words, but he makes repeated reference to *the* covenant of grace, this covenant being given to Abraham. At the same time, he makes reference to the *new* covenant in Christ. On the whole his argument is more cautious than many in that he appeals to "the organic unity of the covenants of God" (p. 100) and to the fact that all of the redemptive Old Testament covenants "were made with believers and with their seed—without exception" (p. 102). He takes care not to go beyond the evidence, so it is hard to disagree with what he says. My question, however, is whether this more modest approach, keeping closer to the affirmations of Scripture than many traditional covenant theologians, provides a sufficient basis for the desired conclusions about infant baptism.

The traditional argument is that infants are included because the new covenant is simply the one Abrahamic covenant of grace. Sinclair Ferguson's more nuanced claim (if I have understood him correctly) is that a continuity between the covenants points to the inclusion of children. This claim is far more plausible than the traditional one, but at the same yields more modest fruit. One might say that it points to the likelihood of the inclusion of children in the new covenant rather than proving it conclusively.

Related to this is the broader problem that I have with covenant theology. It takes the covenant theme as an overarching paradigm for the interpretation of Scripture. With the Old Testament this works quite well, since the covenant theme is clearly prominent throughout the Testament. With the New Testament it does not work so well since the covenant theme, though certainly present, does not have nearly as central a role in New Testament theology as in Old Testament theology.

BAPTISM AND CIRCUMCISION

Fundamental to covenant theology and to Sinclair Ferguson's essay is the claim that baptism has replaced circumcision as the sacrament of initiation into the new covenant. There are a number of problems with this.

First, the New Testament nowhere explicitly links baptism with the theme of covenant. Ironically the link *is* made with the Lord's Supper, in all four accounts of its institution—but not with baptism. Sinclair Ferguson attempts to find such a link. The institution of baptism in Matthew 28 "echoes the history of covenantal redemption" (p. 89) and "expresses the fulfillment of all God's covenant promises" (p. 89). This is certainly a valid exercise in interrelating themes across the Testaments. It falls short, however, of demonstrating an intimate link between baptism and covenant such that the latter is the hermeneutical key for interpreting the former. If that were true, it is surprising that the New Testament writers *never* make the link.

The same observations apply to the statement that 1 Corinthians 10:4 and 1 Peter 3:20-21 both refer to Old Testament events of covenantal significance (p. 98). That may be true, but neither Paul nor Peter saw fit to draw attention to the fact. I do not wish to deny any linkage between baptism and covenant. I do wonder why this linkage should be so fundamental to the interpretation of baptism and infant baptism when the New Testament writers fail to make *any* mention of it.

Not only does the New Testament never link baptism with the covenant, it also never portrays it as the replacement for circumcision. The only passage that links the two together in any way (Col 2:10-11), does not state that the one has replaced the other. The most convincing evidence that it has not is Paul's complete failure to mention this in his opposition to the Judaizers. While recognizing other issues were at stake the fact remains that from a covenant theology perspective it is nonsense to suggest that baptized Christians be circumcised. You have already received the sacrament of initiation into the covenant of grace. Circumcision is superfluous. While Paul opposed the circumcision of Gentile believers, he never suggested that Jews should cease to circumcise their children. Indeed he even had Timothy circumcised (Acts 16:3). That is odd if the covenant theology approach is correct. The first occasion known to us where a parallel is drawn between baptism and circumcision comes with Cyprian, two hundred years after Paul.[1] If the New Testament position really is that baptism simply replaces circumcision, this silence (in the New Testament itself as well as the intervening years) is odd.

On the one hand, Sinclair Ferguson states that baptism "functions in relationship to the new covenant in Christ in a manner analogous

---

[1]*Epistola* 64.2-5 (*ANF* 5:353-54, where it is numbered as 58).

to the function of [circumcision] in the Abrahamic covenant" and "has the same symbolic significance in relationship to fellowship with God as did circumcision" (p. 87). On the other hand he does not claim that "the two signs are equivalent in every respect" (p. 87), although they "share the same core symbolism" and "point to the same promise" (p. 87). It is true that they are the sacraments of initiation into the old and new covenants respectively. It is also true that a considerable degree of continuity exists between the two covenants, though by no means all will concede the extent of continuity claimed by covenant theology. It is also true (and acknowledged by Ferguson) that there is a significant degree of discontinuity between the two covenants—and I would say a greater degree of discontinuity than is conceded by covenant theology. The upshot of this is that it is not illegitimate to draw parallels and make comparisons between circumcision and baptism. Still, it is not safe to draw theological conclusions about baptism from such comparisons unless these are also supported by the testimony of the New Testament.

THEOLOGY OF BAPTISM

My problems with Sinclair Ferguson's essay lie as much with the theology of baptism as with the specific issue of infant baptism. After all, I agree with him that the baptism of babies is a legitimate option for Christian parents, even if I do not base that argument on an appeal to the covenant or to circumcision. I agree with Sinclair Ferguson, and with Calvin,[2] that many of the Baptist arguments against infant baptism would, if true, apply equally against infant circumcision, which clearly was commanded by God. But I am unhappy with the theology of baptism found in his essay, which in many ways seems distant from the New Testament.

First, key to the argument is the claim that baptism is "a sign and seal of the covenant of grace" (pp. 86-87, 100). It is not just that this claim is made, but rather that it functions as the controlling paradigm

---

[2]John Calvin *Institutes of the Christian Religion* 4.16.9, 20.

for the interpretation of baptism. The terms *sign* and *seal* recur in no less than four of the headings for section two. What is remarkable about this is that section two is titled "Baptism and the Biblical Testimony." Yet nowhere in the Bible is baptism expressly linked to the covenant. Nowhere is baptism referred to as either a sign or a seal. Sinclair Ferguson admits as much, but claims that while "these features are not explicitly attributed to baptism, each is evidently [sic!] true of it" (p. 86). Now I would not wish to affirm that baptism has no connection at all with the new covenant, and I would not wish to deny that it is appropriate to use the word *sign* or *seal* in relation to it. But when these ideas, not found in the New Testament, are used as the *controlling framework* for the exposition of baptism, we are left wondering how faithful the ensuing picture is to the New Testament doctrine of baptism.[3] I am not against systematic theology, the interrelating of doctrines drawing on both Old and New Testaments; but systematic theology always faces the temptation of forcing the biblical material into an alien framework. In this case I see the doctrine of baptism being pressed into a framework that originates not from the clear and direct statements made about baptism in the New Testament but from doctrines of covenant and circumcision that in the New Testament are never explicitly linked with baptism. It is not that these ideas have no part at all to play in the understanding of baptism but that we have no grounds for making them the controlling paradigm for the doctrine.

Related to this is the imposition of another category foreign to the New Testament. Following Calvin and the Reformers, Sinclair Ferguson links baptism with the Word. Doing this enables him to claim that the "proper" function of baptism (as of the Word) is to

---

[3]Calvin differs significantly here. In his chapter on baptism (*Institutes* 4.15) he expounds NT teaching on baptism and appeals to circumcision and covenant only toward the end, when arguing that baptism is not invalidated by unworthy ministers and that women should not baptize (*Institutes* 4.15.16-17, 22). By contrast, in the following chapter, on infant baptism, the two words appear nearly 120 times. While Calvin's defense of infant baptism is similar to that of covenant theology, his basic exposition of baptism is not controlled by the ideas of covenant or circumcision.

display and portray God's grace (p. 113). He affirms the same with a
rich variety of language. Baptism "points" (pp. 89, 90, 91, 92, 112),
"symbolizes" (pp. 91, 99), "signifies" (pp. 89, 90, 91, 92, 95, 99, 100)
and "proclaims" (p. 92). This theme owes much to Reformed theology, little to the New Testament. In the latter baptism is paired not
with the Word but with faith. Why? Because for the New Testament
writers, the prime function of baptism is not to "portray" grace but
(together with faith) to receive it. That is why they (unlike Sinclair
Ferguson) do not stress (or even mention) the idea of baptism as a
sign or symbol.

The instrumental role of baptism in receiving salvation ought
not to need stating, but this aspect of New Testament teaching has
been so widely suppressed in most (not all) evangelical teaching
that it is worth quoting some passages in full. These all portray
baptism not as a symbol pointing to something but as having a role
in the reception of salvation—not of course in opposition to faith
but together with it.

> And Peter said to them, "Repent and be baptized every one of you in
> the name of Jesus Christ for the forgiveness of your sins, and you will
> receive the gift of the Holy Spirit." (Acts 2:38)

> And now why do you wait? Rise and be baptized and wash away
> your sins, calling on his name. (Acts 22:16)

> We were buried therefore with him by baptism into death, in order
> that, just as Christ was raised from the dead by the glory of the Fa-
> ther, we too might walk in newness of life. (Rom 6:4)

> For in Christ Jesus you are all sons of God, through faith. For as
> many of you as were baptized into Christ have put on Christ. (Gal
> 3:26-27)

> Having been buried with [Christ] in baptism, in which you were also
> raised with him through faith in the powerful working of God, who
> raised him from the dead. (Col 2:12)

> Baptism . . . now saves you. (1 Pet 3:21)

All of these passages portray baptism as (not in isolation but together with faith) the means by which we receive the gift of salvation, including forgiveness, union with Christ and the Holy Spirit.[4] This coheres with the pattern of fourfold initiation that I describe in my main essay, whereby becoming a Christian involves repentance, faith, baptism and reception of the Holy Spirit. Because (as we see in Acts) these all came together, the New Testament writers were not embarrassed to attribute salvation to baptism as well as to faith.

Salvation is received by the faith that expresses itself in baptism and by the baptism that is an expression of faith. Of course, attributing this power to bring salvation to baptism separate from faith is an abuse of the New Testament. It is just as surely an abuse of the New Testament to attribute such power to faith in isolation from baptism. In affirming that "one becomes a Christian at baptism" (p. 84) the early Fathers were following the pattern of Acts. To the extent that they may have separated baptism from faith, they departed from that pattern. The New Testament attributes efficacy to believing baptism, not to unbelieving baptism.

Ferguson appears to be pulled in two directions on this question. On the one hand he lays stress throughout on the fact that baptism is a sign and symbol. On the other hand it is not a "bare sign" but "points to and communicates" Christ's presence (p. 92). Ferguson leaves no room in his account for the New Testament idea of baptism as *receiving* Christ, since this is "enjoyed only through faith" (p. 90). The nearest he comes to baptism as receiving is in his rather tortured expression that both baptism and the preached word are "means by which the Spirit can and does communicate to receptive faith the divine blessings the signs signify" (p. 93).

He only states that baptism is more than a bare sign by teaching that it has a "rich *objective* significance" (p. 90), not by recognizing that baptism plays a role in the reception of salvation.

---

[4]As is expounded by G. R. Beasley-Murray, *Baptism in the New Testament* (London: Macmillan, 1962), pp. 263-305, on the basis of the preceding exegetical work (pp. 93-262).

Today we face the problem that Western Christians have for centuries separated faith and baptism and treated them as alternatives. Do we become Christians by faith or baptism? This question would have puzzled New Testament Christians, who would have replied that it is by the faith that expresses itself in baptism and by the baptism that is an expression of faith.

INFANT BAPTISM

But what of children? I object not so much to Sinclair Ferguson's affirmation of infant baptism as to the means by which he justifies it. He demonstrates a continuity between the covenants and shows how in the Old Testament "divine covenants in redemptive history were made with believers and their seed—without exception" (p. 102). There is a "continuity of administration" (p. 104) that points to the baptism of infants.

The weakness of the covenant theology case at this point is that, as Ferguson himself affirms, God's grace is "differently administered" in the two Testaments (p. 101). Women were not circumcised, but they are baptized. Also, the old covenant was not just with a family but with a nation, and in this post-Constantinian age no one seriously denies that this has changed. The people of God in the Old Testament were an elect nation, while the people of God in the New Testament form not an elect nation but the elect from all nations. Thus even were we to concede that in Old and New Testaments there is only one covenant of grace, that baptism does simply replace circumcision and that baptism is the sacrament of initiation into the new covenant, important differences remain in administration which affect the question of who receives baptism. Given these differences, it is far from inevitable that children will be baptized because they were circumcised.

I do admit that the argument from the continuity of the covenants serves at the very least to give plausibility to the concept of infant baptism and indeed to impose a burden of proof upon those who would exclude it. On its own, however, I see it as offering less than conclusive proof. I am not persuaded that it demands (rather than permits) the baptism of infants. Nor were the early Christians so persuaded, since they accepted (so I have argued in my main essay) the validity of delaying the baptism of Christian children.

A final thought. The early Fathers clearly believed that baptism did something, which is why they took care about whom they gave it to. This has been compared to the bestowal of nationality.[5] Perhaps baptism could be compared to a Christian passport. Circumcision can certainly be viewed in many ways as a passport—and one which, unlike modern passports, cannot be stolen and does not need renewing every ten years, though it is more embarrassing to be required to produce it! Circumcision can be seen as the token of citizenship in the people of God. Baptism is also the means of entry into the people of God (Acts 2:41) and has always been seen as such by Jews and Muslims. It is not when a Jew or Muslim talks about believing in Jesus, but when they are baptized, that they are seen to have turned from their previous religion and joined the Christian community. Baptism played the same role for the early Christians in New Testament times and beyond, serving as the point of entry into the people of God. Regarding the baptism or nonbaptism of children, this might be compared to the way in which children sometimes have passports of their own, sometimes travel on their parents' passports.

---

[5]I am indebted to Gerald Bray for this analogy.

Concluding Response

Sinclair B. Ferguson

WHILE OUR DISCUSSION MAY HAVE REACHED AN IMPASSE, it has brought to the surface some of the important theological and exegetical differences underlying diversity in baptismal practice. Here I can only sketch a response to Professor Lane and Professor Ware. It will focus chiefly on the role of God's covenant and also the relationship between baptism and circumcision.

COVENANT PERSPECTIVE

Covenantal nature of the gospel. Paradoxically, Professor Ware, a credobaptist, seems more comfortable with the covenantal nature of the gospel than Professor Lane. The latter wishes to marginalize the role of the covenant in the New Testament in general and for baptism in particular.

Professor Lane admits several of my affirmations: (1) infants may be baptized; (2) baptism and covenant can be linked; (3) baptism may be called a sign and seal. (The latter two points are reluctantly [?] conceded in the circumlocution: "I would not wish to affirm that baptism has no connection with the new covenant and I would not wish to deny that it is appropriate to use the word *sign* or *seal* in relation to it," p. 125.)

To reject the centrality of the covenantal paradigm in the New

Testament is, in my view, to read the Bible with Western eyes, backward from the present, and to fail to be sensitive to its fundamental textures when read forward from the Old Testament.

1. The authors of the New Testament were, almost without exception, Jews, steeped in the Old Testament (or Covenant!). They saw *everything* through covenantal eyes.[1]

2. Luke (the Gentile) begins his Gospel with a recognition that its whole narrative stands under a covenant rubric (Lk 1:72). Indeed Christ himself embodies (is!) the "new covenant" (Lk 22:20). He is a covenant Christ. The reason the term *covenant* as such recedes is because it is now personally embodied in the person of Christ himself.

3. The gospel itself is structured by the distinct covenant pattern (an indicative grounding an imperative).

4. Christ's whole work falls under the rubric of a covenant mediator (Hebrews).

5. Christians are described in transferred covenant terms (saints, called, elect, heirs, people of God, adopted, temple, bride, real circumcision, righteous, blessed, etc.).

6. The apostles are, by definition, "ministers of a new covenant" (2 Cor 3:6).

To call the entire twenty-seven-book collection of testimony to the gospel "The New Testament or Covenant" is simply to summarize and acknowledge the force of these points. I am not arguing that covenant is the *only* organizing principle in the Scriptures. But it permeates everything in the New Testament. Insofar as this is the case, those present at Pentecost saw baptism through lenses already tinted with a covenant perspective.

---

[1]Cf. the judicious (but representative) comments of Herman N. Ridderbos, *Paul: An Outline of His Theology*, trans. J. R. de Witt (Grand Rapids: Eerdmans, 1975), p. 335.

Exegetical-theological grounding. Curiously Professor Lane offers no substantial *exegetical-theological* grounding for (1) his notion that infant baptism is legitimate *but* not mandated, nor for (2) his method to determine the choice to baptize or not.

Rather than support dual practice, the early Christian writings on baptism seem to me to express the struggling efforts of pastors (as theologians once were!) to bring some semblance of coherence and order to a church whose practice was confused by a fear of post-baptismal sin and influenced by increasing sacramentalism. Their response, to use Professor Lane's own terminology, was "a question of strategy rather than principle" (p. 147). Had dual practice been apostolic, later writers would have appealed directly and specifically to it as both a de facto reality and a de jure doctrine. Variety bordering on confusion is not a sound argument for dual practice. The church fathers are far from suggesting the possibility that children can travel either on their own passport (infant baptism) or on their parents' passport (delayed baptism). Perhaps, if they ever contemplated it, they realized it would simply add to the confusion.

It remains far from clear how the infant baptism implied in this dual practice position comports with Professor Lane's "high" view of the *instrumentality* of baptism in salvation. Further, the view suggests that the true "dual practice code" has been somehow hidden throughout church history. A chase around early church history has its moments of interest, but there is a whiff of *The Da Vinci Code* in the idea that dual practice was known by the apostles but committed neither to Scripture nor clearly through the episcopate! So I continue to regard this dual practice position as unsubstantiated, while happily enjoying the personal privilege of baptizing both converts to Christ and the infants of believers!

The Relationship of Circumcision and Baptism

Both Professor Lane and Professor Ware downplay the relationship between baptism and circumcision. A number of points here should be noted.

Redemption history's narrative pattern. As already indicated, when the narrative of redemptive history is followed through, a clear pattern emerges. Each divine covenant was accompanied by a physical representation. Quite apart from the specific language of Romans 4:11, it can be demonstrated that these physical representations functioned as "signs" and "seals." This language is therefore justifiably appropriated to any rite which shares a parallel covenantal function.

Functional levels of circumcision. It is also argued that since circumcision functioned at two levels, ethnic and spiritual, while baptism functions only at the spiritual level, it "simply is not meant to be seen as parallel to circumcision" (p. 114), nor "as the replacement for circumcision" (p. 123).

Circumcision and baptism function symbolically within the context of their own covenant. The irreducible, central significance to every administration of circumcision was the promise "I will . . . be God to you" (Gen 17:7), which when received in faith led to justification. It had this significance whether it was applied to an old man who had come to faith or to an eight-day-old infant. The word, not the faith of the recipient, gave circumcision its meaning.

Thus circumcision, like baptism, pointed primarily to "spiritual" reality—the very point Paul makes in Romans 4:11—and as such could be administered to infants. The core significance of circumcision was analogous to that of baptism.

While the outworking of the covenant of circumcision took place largely within a single nation, the Old Testament as a whole and the prophetic writings in particular stress the unacceptability of being circumcised yet not coming to faith (e.g., Jer 6:10; 9:25-26). This is not a novel perspective that arises only from within the new covenant. It further underlines that the central meaning of circumcision, whether in adults or children, was the divine relationship.

Credobaptists' necessary dislocation. The credobaptist must dislocate circumcision from baptism. To allow them to coalesce is virtually to acknowledge covenant continuity and to concede a spiritual center to the circumcision of infants. Hence two arguments are raised:

BAPTISM: THREE VIEWS

1. It is claimed that baptism is never said to replace circumcision. Not quite in so many words, but several passages indicate their functional equivalence with respect to their own covenants. For example, the baptized are described by Paul as "the true circumcision" (Phil 3:3). Not circumcision but baptism marks the true offspring of Abraham (Gal 3:27-29). These statements imply that now the former sign of initiation (circumcision) has been replaced by the new sign (baptism).

Further, whatever the exegetical intricacies of Colossians 2:8-12, no reading of this passage "works" unless it recognizes that both circumcision and baptism point to one and the same reality. Thus even Jewett in his groundbreaking antipaedobaptist polemic conceded that "Circumcision may fairly be said to be the Old Testament counterpart of Christian Baptism. So far the Reformed argument, in our judgment, is biblical. In this sense, baptism, to quote the Heidelberg Catechism, 'occupies the place of circumcision in the New Testament.'"[2]

In Colossians 2:11-12 both circumcision ("you were circumcised") and baptism ("having been buried with him in baptism") point to "the circumcision of Christ" or "the Christ-circumcision," that is (in my view) to *the work of Christ on the cross*[3] which is applied to us by the Spirit. Baptism (or circumcision) *first* points away from the recipient—not at the recipient—to Christ. This of course is why the same sign, with the same significance, can be given to both an adult and a child.

At the end of the day the credobaptist must resort to the false dichotomy that in adult circumcision righteousness *and* ethnicity were signified, while infant circumcision signifies *only* ethnicity (since

---

[2]Paul K. Jewett, *Infant Baptism and the Covenant of Grace* (Grand Rapids: Eerdmans, 1978), p. 89.

[3]For this view, see, among others, C. F. D. Moule, *The Epistles of Paul the Apostle to the Colossians and to Philemon: An Introduction and Commentary,* The Cambridge Greek New Testament Commentary (London: Cambridge University Press, 1957), p. 96; James D. G. Dunn, *The Epistles to the Colossians and Philemon: A Commentary on the Greek Text,* New International Greek Testament Commentary (Grand Rapids: Eerdmans, 1996), p. 158; P. T. O'Brien, *Colossians, Philemon,* Word Biblical Commentary (Waco, Tex.: Word, 1982), 44:116-17.

the child could not have justifying faith). In the new covenant, ethnicity is no part of the significance of baptism and is abrogated. Only faith remains. Therefore only professing believers are baptized. But this puts asunder what God joined together in circumcision. Such a false starting place inevitably leads to a false conclusion.

A frequently unspoken concern in credobaptism is the assumption that it alone makes for a "purer" or more "spiritual" church; paedobaptism by definition pollutes the church's bloodstream. The statistics tracing membership absence from worship in credobaptist churches (at least in the U.S.) surely underline the fact that only gospel reality, not sacramental administration, encourages purity.

2. Professors Lane and Ware both imply a familiar argument against baptism "replacing" circumcision:

Major Premise: If baptism replaced circumcision, the apostles would have said:[4] "Circumcision has replaced baptism; *therefore* circumcision is no longer necessary."

Minor Premise: The apostles did not say this.

Conclusion: Therefore circumcision did not replace baptism.

This argument is flawed, logically, historically and pastorally.

- The major premise contains an unproven assumption without logical proof or historical evidence. The reasoning is theologically and pastorally flawed. To say "the inaugural sign has changed from circumcision to baptism" would not have dealt with the underlying theological issue, the gospel of grace itself.

- Late medieval theology illustrates that it is possible for those who believe that baptism replaces circumcision to be just as confused as the Judaizers were about the nature of grace. The *theological* and *pastoral* issues could not have been resolved merely by saying "baptism has replaced circumcision," but only by clearly articulating the gospel and its implications (hence Galatians!).

---

[4]This argument is frequently employed with reference to the decree of the "Council of Jerusalem" in Acts 15:1-29.

It is further objected to seeing baptism as a "visible word" that Scripture associates baptism *with faith,* not *with the word* (pp. 125-26). This is a demonstrably false antithesis. It ignores the fact that "faith" is always shorthand for "faith in the Christ made known in his revelatory word." For "faith comes from hearing, and hearing through the word of Christ" (Rom 10:17). Faith is never separated from the word about Christ. Furthermore water functions as baptism only because the word invests it with a meaning to which faith responds. Water without the word is . . . water. Because of the word, water becomes baptism—a visible word indeed, pointing to the Christ faith receives.

Space constraints prevent fuller comment on Professor Lane's view that the apostles "attribute salvation to baptism as well as to faith."(p. 127). Paul would not have written "Christ did not send me to baptize *but* to preach the gospel" (1 Cor 1:17) had he related baptism to salvation in this way. The older formulation suggesting a language of sacramental union between the sign and the thing signified remains a more satisfactory account. Better to say that it is by Christ himself we are saved as faith responds to him who is signified and sealed to us in baptism.

Much more might be said. Here it remains only to express appreciation to Professors Tony Lane and Bruce Ware for their essays and responses and for the benefit to the church of their other publications. Likewise, with my colleagues, I would like to salute the memory of the late Professor David Wright who both initiated this project and persevered with it. Only affection for David and his kindness to me since my student days would have persuaded me—as he knew!—to step into the lions' den of baptism with Professors Lane and Ware. Our joint project is immeasurably the poorer without his intended lengthy contribution to the discussion in his capacity as editor and umpire. My own hope was that, having given so much of his attention as a scholar to historical questions about baptism, David himself might find his way into the den and point us to the way out. Instead for him the baptism question is, surely, now finally resolved to his complete satisfaction. Those of us who are still *in via* continue to think of him with deep affection. He was an outstandingly good scholar, a man of immense erudition and exacting standards, and—best of all—he served Christ and his baptized people faithfully.

3

DUAL-PRACTICE BAPTISM VIEW

Anthony N. S. Lane

MY TASK IN THIS CHAPTER IS CONSIDERABLY easier than that of my two colleagues, and not just because they have graciously allowed me the privilege of defending the correct view. I also have the advantage of occupying the middle position, which means that they will have argued at length for the validity of baptizing babies and for the value of deferring baptism, both of which I believe in. In this chapter we will begin with the process of becoming a Christian in the New Testament, go on to ask whether the apostolic church baptized babies and conclude with a discussion of some of the theological issues relating to the baptism of babies.

Please permit me first to begin with a word of personal testimony. I was born to nonchurchgoing parents. At the age of three I was baptized in an Anglican church, at my grandmother's urging. Apparently I cried out, "He's not going to pour that water over me!" For a time I thought of this as early evidence of theological discernment, but I now regard it as the folly of youth. The price that my mother had to pay for having me baptized was a promise to seek confirmation. This she did, and it turned us into churchgoers. Much later in life she moved beyond that into a living personal faith.

In due course I myself was converted and went on to study theology. I gave little thought to infant baptism, though I saw no point in it. Then while using a commentary by two high-churchmen in my study of Romans chapter 6, it suddenly dawned on me that baptism made perfect sense if confined to believers. I discussed this with friends, who told me that the best defence of infant baptism was Pierre Marcel's *The Biblical Doctrine of Infant Baptism: The Sacrament of the Covenant of Grace.*[1] I read it eagerly but decided that the apparently logical argument was flawed by a number of unacknowledged gaps, so Marcel made a Baptist of me. For over thirty years I have belonged to baptistic churches, and my children were not baptized as babies.

At a later stage I read George Beasley-Murray's *Baptism in the New Testament.*[2] This Baptist author persuaded me that New Testament baptism was not so much believers' baptism as converts' baptism. Thinking about this made me realize that Baptist and paedobaptist practice are alike modifications of this. At the same time I was concerned about the fact that my children appeared to be believers but were not yet baptized, a situation that I could not square with the New Testament. The suggestion that such children should take communion until they were old enough for baptism struck me as hopelessly confused. So Beasley-Murray (with help) moved me away from the Baptist position.

The purpose of this narrative is not just to demonstrate that I am a cussed individual who always reacts against things but also to show that the position argued in this essay comes from having lived and thought within the two opposing positions and having myself found both of them to be wanting.

CHRISTIAN INITIATION IN THE NEW TESTAMENT
How does one become a Christian? Our discussion of baptism must begin with this fundamental question. What must I do to be saved?

---

[1]Pierre Marcel, *The Biblical Doctrine of Infant Baptism: The Sacrament of the Covenant of Grace* (London: James Clarke, 1953).

[2]George R. Beasley-Murray, *Baptism in the New Testament* (London: Macmillan, 1962).

What needs to happen when someone wishes to respond to the gospel? Or to use the jargon, what is Christian initiation? One way to answer this question is to look at the Acts of the Apostles, where we see the apostles preaching the gospel to unbelievers. In particular fourteen passages narrate how evangelists tell enquirers how to respond or provide a reasonably full account of the conversion of a person or group.[3]

If we look at these passages and ask what was expected to happen, we find four things that repeatedly occur: repentance, faith, baptism and reception of the Holy Spirit. All four are not mentioned every time, but a clear fourfold pattern emerges.[4] Faith is mentioned ten times and is found in a variant reading in an eleventh passage (Acts 8:37). Apart from Peter's address in Acts 3 (which the police interrupted), the only place where faith is missing is in two accounts of Paul's conversion (Acts 9:17-18; 22:14-16), though it may safely be assumed that his conversion did involve faith.[5] Baptism is also mentioned ten times, the exceptions including the incomplete sermon of Acts 3. The other omissions are Acts 15:7-9, referring to the conversion of Cornelius who was in fact baptized (Acts 10:47-48), the sermon on Mars Hill (Acts 17:30-34) and Paul's account of his own teaching in Acts 20:20-21.

That all four things are not mentioned every time shows that Luke was not a pedant, not that all four things did not happen each time. This can be seen from multiple accounts of the same event (conversions of Paul and Cornelius) where different things are mentioned each time. When the apostles suspected that one of these was missing, they took care to remedy the defect (Acts 8:15-17, 20-23; 19:1-7).

---

[3]Acts 2:37-41; 3:17-21; 8:12-17, 36-39; 9:17-18; 10:43-48; 11:15-18; 15:7-9; 16:14-15, 30-34; 17:30-34; 19:1-7; 20:20-21; 22:14-16.

[4]James D. G. Dunn, *Baptism in the Holy Spirit* (London: SCM Press, 1970), p. 91, sees three elements in Christian initiation: repentance, baptism and the gift of the Spirit. He then states that repentance and faith are "opposite sides of the same coin." It makes more sense to speak of four elements, as does David Pawson, *The Normal Christian Birth* (London: Hodder & Stoughton, 1989), pp. 9-90.

[5]In Acts 26:15-18 Paul is instructed at his conversion to preach sanctification by faith.

This picture coheres with what we see in the rest of the New Testament, where faith and baptism are like the clichéd two sides of a coin. Baptism is a part of Christian initiation by which people become Christians, but this is not baptism without faith. Baptism is also part of the gospel message. In the Great Commission of Matthew 28:19-20 baptism is commanded, but faith is not even mentioned! For the New Testament writers *faith* means "faith confessed in baptism" and *baptism* means "baptism as a confession of faith." They thought of faith and baptism as a unity, not just on theoretical grounds but because in actual practice they came together. It was easy therefore for them to glide unselfconsciously from talking about the one to talking about the other. A few examples will suffice:

> In Christ Jesus you are all sons of God, through faith. For as many of you as were baptized into Christ have put on Christ. (Gal 3:26-27 ESV)

> In him you were also circumcised, in the putting off of the sinful nature, not with a circumcision done by the hands of men but with the circumcision done by Christ, having been buried with him in baptism and raised with him through your faith in the power of God, who raised him from the dead. (Colossians 2:11-12 NIV)

Perhaps the most striking example lies in the very structure of Romans. In Romans 1—5 Paul develops his doctrine of justification by faith. In Romans 6 he unselfconsciously turns to a discussion of baptism. Has he completely changed the subject? No. The faith that justifies is the faith that gave birth to baptism at conversion. The baptism by which they were buried with Christ is the baptism with which they expressed their faith at their conversion. A single reality is being discussed from two different angles, as is seen from the blending of faith and confession of Christ (in baptism) in Romans 10:9-10.

New Testament converts' baptism and infant baptism. Do we need to continue? Surely it is abundantly clear that the practice of the apostles as recorded in Acts was believers' baptism, the baptism of those who had come to faith and repentance, the position taken by Baptists today. So it is commonly understood, but this is not quite true. What we see in Acts is not *believers'* baptism but *converts'* baptism.[6] People are baptized at the point of their conversion.

Baptism is clearly seen as part of the initial response to the gospel in Acts. Baptism was an essential part of Christian initiation. People were baptized immediately on their conversion, on the very same day, with only one exception. The exception is the Philippian jailer, who was baptized the same night! Baptism was not optional. It was not left to the conscience of the individual believer. It was not delayed until the convert's genuineness was proved. Instead it was part of the gospel message. So in his epistles Paul can assume that his readers have all been baptized (1 Cor 12:13; Eph 4:4-6).

If apostolic baptism was converts' baptism, does that not exclude the baptism of babies? Not necessarily. People were baptized at the point of their conversion. But what happened to their children? What happened to the existing babies and children of those earliest converts? In particular were they baptized with their parents? What happened to the children subsequently born to them? How were they initiated? Were they baptized at birth or at some subsequent stage? Unfortunately neither Luke nor any other New Testament writer gives an unequivocal, explicit answer to this question. Whatever did happen to these children, of one thing we can be certain. They did not receive the converts' baptism described in Acts. Whether they were baptized that day or at the age of five, twelve or eighteen, their baptism was an adaptation of adult converts' baptism to the changed situation of those brought up in a Christian home. The New Testament practice and doctrine of baptism is that of converts' baptism, and *however* the children of those converts were treated would be a modification of that.

Scholars have sometimes suggested that this did not become an issue until the second generation of the church, but that is far from

[6]As is shown by Beasley-Murray, *Baptism in the New Testament,* e.g., pp. 393-94.

the truth. The New Testament church was not a student Christian Union of youngsters who had yet to settle down and have families. The three thousand converts on the day of Pentecost must have had many children of every age. Whether or not to baptize was an issue that had to be decided *that day.* How was it decided?

DID THE APOSTOLIC CHURCH BAPTIZE BABIES?

A seismological approach. Traditionally this question has been answered by considering all of the evidence available from New Testament times, which is notoriously ambiguous. I have suggested an alternative "seismological" approach.[7] Without leaving their own laboratories, seismologists in New York can observe and measure earthquakes that take place in Los Angeles. How do they do this? They can tell what has happened in California by its effects two to three thousand miles away. In a similar manner I would suggest that we can deduce what was the situation in apostolic times by its effects two to three hundred years later.

The beginning of infant baptism. When did infant baptism, the baptism of those too young to speak for themselves, begin? This historical question was argued at some length (but inconclusively) in a famous exchange between two German scholars, Joachim Jeremias, who defended the apostolic origin of infant baptism, and Kurt Aland, who denied it.[8] The evidence before the end of the second century is so meager and ambiguous that it is widely accepted that a firm verdict is not possible. It may be helpful therefore, in seeking to answer the question, to work backward using our seismological approach: that is, to start from a time in church history where it is clear what happened and to work back from that point to New Testament times.

---

[7]A. N. S. Lane, "Did the Apostolic Church Baptise Babies? A Seismological Approach," *Tyndale Bulletin* 55, no. 1 (2004): 109-30. This section is an abbreviation of that article.
[8]Joachim Jeremias, *Infant Baptism in the First Four Centuries* (London: SCM Press, 1960); Kurt Aland, *Did the Early Church Baptize Infants?* (London: SCM Press, 1963); Joachim Jeremias, *The Origins of Infant Baptism* (London: SCM Press, 1963). Kurt Aland, *Die Stellung der Kinder in den frühen christlichen Gemeinden—und ihre Taufe* (Munich: Chr. Kaiser, 1967), has not been translated.

The evidence becomes clearer as the centuries go by. In line with the principle of working from what is plain to what is obscure, we will begin with the third century, move on to the fourth and fifth, go back to the second century and end with the first century.

Third-century evidence. For the third century we have five major sources of information: the *Apostolic Tradition*, Tertullian, Cyprian, Origen and inscriptions on Christian tombstones. It is important to distinguish different types of evidence.[9] Sermons and other writings contain exhortations either to baptize or not to baptize babies. These testify to the views of the authors and show what views were considered acceptable but do not in themselves prove that anyone actually followed the advice given. Literary biographical information or inscriptions offer evidence as to when specific individuals were baptized. In between these two types are church orders and other works regulating practice. These do not give hard statistical information but are clearly a far more reliable indicator as to what actually happened than are exhortatory sermons.

The first of our witnesses, the *Apostolic Tradition,* is the hardest to place. Many hold that Hippolytus composed it at Rome in about A.D. 215. More recently scholars have argued that the text as known today (in various translations from the Greek) is a composite work derived from different sources from the second to fourth centuries. On this understanding, the earliest core of the work dates, maybe, from the mid-second century.[10] Either way, the earliest material can be seen as evidence of what was happening at the beginning of the third century at the very latest. Chapters sixteen to twenty-three describe the ceremony of baptism. This is still clearly geared to new converts. The only mention of infants comes in three sentences. After the statement that candidates are to be baptized naked, it is stated that the first to be baptized should be the little children. These should

---

[9]I am indebted to David Wright for this point.

[10]Paul F. Bradshaw, Maxwell E. Johnson and L. Edward Phillips, *The Apostolic Tradition: A Commentary,* ed. H. W. Attridge, Hermeneia (Minneapolis: Fortress, 2002), pp. 1-6, 13-15.

speak for themselves if they can, otherwise one of their family should speak for them.[11] These chapters in general, and the instructions about small children in particular, are found in the earliest core of the document.[12]

The text describes a ceremony designed for adults in which small children are included. Some children could answer for themselves, but some infants were too young to answer. Finding children here (and elsewhere) fitted into an essentially adult ceremony should occasion no surprise since the practice of baptism described in Acts is *converts'* baptism. *Whatever* happened to Christian children at whatever age, it would involve adapting that process to include them.

One cannot say how long children had been included by the time of the *Apostolic Tradition*, except that this practice is unlikely to have been a recent innovation. The practice presumably reflects the reality of what was happening then and included the baptism of little children both at an age when they could speak and at an earlier stage when they could not. This is an account of a regular baptismal service and so *does not refer to the emergency baptism of dying babies*. While one cannot deduce that all Christians were having their infants baptized, the document is clear evidence that some infants (too young to answer for themselves) were being baptized.

At the turn of the third century Tertullian, at Carthage in North Africa, wrote a work titled *On Baptism*. Here he urges that baptism should be delayed, especially for little children.[13] Tertullian opposes the baptism of children, including those too young to speak for themselves (i.e., infants) and so needing sponsors. Tertullian's counsel for delay also means that he is opposing the "regular" baptism of infants, not the emergency baptism of dying infants. A superficial

---

[11]Ibid., *Didache* 21.4, pp. 112-13. This material is found in the Sahidic, Arabic and Ethiopic translations.

[12]Ibid., pp. 15, 124.

[13]*De baptismo* 18, probably from around the year 200 and available in English translation in *Tertullian's Homily on Baptism,* edited with an introduction, translation and commentary by Ernest Evans (London: SPCK, 1964), pp. 36-41, commentary on pp. 101-6; *ANF* 3:677-78; PL 1:1220-22; CCL 1:292-93).

reading might portray him as a proto-Baptist fighting the emerging practice of infant baptism, but the situation is somewhat different.

One argument Tertullian does not use against child baptism is that it is a recent innovation. In the ancient world novelty and innovation were regarded as something bad, not desirable. Elsewhere Tertullian in particular argued at length that truth is ancient and goes back to the apostles while heresy is recent.[14] He would hardly have neglected to use that argument here if he could have. Tertullian was converted to the Christian faith by the mid-190s. At that time he would have known people who had been Christians for some time. If infant baptism had been unknown at the beginning of the African church or in the middle of the second century (whichever is later), Tertullian would have known and mentioned that fact.

Tertullian urges against hurrying children to baptism while they are in the age of innocence and need not hasten to the forgiveness of sins. What motivates Tertullian here is the fear of postbaptismal sin. Baptism, it was believed, washes away all previous sin. But what of sins committed after baptism? Finding forgiveness for these was not so straightforward. Given that fact, it was prudent to time one's baptism so as to derive the maximum benefit. So, in the same passage, Tertullian urges the unmarried and widows to delay baptism until they are married, and thus safely out of temptation's way.

Tertullian here is urging delay, but he is seeking a change of *established* practice and does so because of his beliefs about postbaptismal sin. Baptism was like a trump card—it is important to play it at the right time. Tertullian believed that baptizing children was inexpedient; he did not claim that it was illegitimate, irregular or invalid. In short, Tertullian had no objection *in principle* to infant baptism. This was a question of strategy rather than principle. Tertullian bears witness to the fact that little children were being baptized for reasons other than emergency baptism. His own exhortation that baptism be

---

[14]E.g., *De praescriptione haereticorum* 31, 34-35, from roughly the same time as *De baptismo*. See <www.newadvent.org/fathers/0311.htm>, and for Latin original <www.tertullian.org/latin/de_praescriptione_haereticorum.htm>.

delayed is not itself proof that his advice was followed, but such proof is found elsewhere.

A generation after Tertullian, Cyprian, bishop of Carthage and an admirer of Tertullian, also wrote about baptism. His *Letter* 64 to Fidus, written in the early 250s, discusses the question of infant baptism in the light of controversy and reports the conclusions of a council of African bishops held at Carthage. The issues have changed since the time of Tertullian. Now the only point in question is whether or not to delay baptism until the child is eight days old, following the Old Testament pattern with circumcision. Various arguments were invoked in the debate, the most imaginative being that babies' feet are too repugnant at birth to receive the kiss of peace![15]

Some scholars have suggested that this debate focused on the appropriate time for the emergency baptism of sick children, but surely the appropriate time in such cases is when the emergency strikes. Infant mortality was by no means confined to the first few days of life. It is hard to believe that considerations of the repugnance of the newborn would really cause delay with a baby that was about to die. As Cyprian reports, the council resolved that newborn babies should not be hindered from being baptized.

While the council may have spoken, it does not follow that all African Christians had their babies baptized. The existence of a serious controversy between baptism at birth and baptism on the eighth day means that a significant number of Christians must have been having their babies baptized. Further evidence for this is the practice of infant communion,[16] which presupposes infant baptism. Infant baptism was seen as bringing the forgiveness of *original* sin. In the fifth century this was used to argue that *all* Christian babies should be baptized, but that did not happen in the third century, the fear of postbaptismal sin proving more powerful than the fear of original sin.

---

[15]*Epistola* 64:2-5 (PL 3:1013-19; CCL 3C:418-25; *ANF* 5:353-54 [numbered 58]; FC 51:216-19; ACW 46:109-12).

[16]Cyprian *De lapsis* 9, 25, see Cyprian, *De Lapsis, English and Latin*, trans. Maurice Bévenot, Oxford Early Christian Texts (Oxford: Clarendon Press, 1971).

Origen was a contemporary of Cyprian who lived in Alexandria. He, like Cyprian, justifies infant baptism by an appeal to the doctrine of original sin. Newborn babies are not pure and innocent. Origen claims that infant baptism is a tradition from the apostles.[17] Born into a Christian family in about A.D. 185, Origen did not of course have any privileged access to apostolic times, so his belief would require that infant baptism was an established practice at least by the last quarter of the second century. We cannot be certain whether Origen was himself baptized as a baby, but there can be no serious doubt as to whether infant baptism was at that time being practiced. Origen in his youth would have known people who had been Christians for sixty or seventy years. If *none* of these had been baptized as babies, it is most unlikely that he would have claimed that the practice was apostolic. Indeed it could be argued that Origen's writings show that infant baptism was practiced shortly after A.D. 100.

Too many discussions of this topic play down the significance of tradition. I once heard a lady on the radio tell how her grandmother had described to her seeing Napoleon go into exile in 1815. That event was almost two hundred years ago yet I have heard a secondhand account of it. People in the Congo today heard from their grandparents a firsthand account of David Livingstone's death (1873). Theology can of course change subtly over the years; but a simple fact like whether or not babies were baptized can easily be remembered. Polycarp knew from his own experience whether or not babies were baptized in the late apostolic age. It is unlikely that he and others took this information to the grave with them. This does not preclude changes taking place, but it does mean that informed Christians at the end of the second century were not as ignorant of early practice, as is usually assumed. Of course they often had no reason to divulge this information or indeed good reason not to.

---

[17]*Commentary on Romans* 5.9 on 6.5-7. See Origen, *Commentary on the Epistle to the Romans, Books 1—5,* trans. Thomas P. Scheck, FC 103 (Washington, D.C.: Catholic University of America Press, 2001).

Had Tertullian, for example, had any reason to suppose that the practice of infant baptism was introduced after the time of the apostles, he had every motive to say so. Where Origen makes claims that infant baptism is from the apostles, either he is lying or he knows of no time when babies were not being baptized. This is not to claim that *all* babies were being baptized at any point, but rather that at no time accessible to these writers was the practice unknown. If that is so, the baptism of babies must go back at the very least to about A.D. 150, if not to the beginning of the second century.

Given the geographical diversity of Hippolytus (Rome),[18] Tertullian (Carthage) and Origen (Alexandria), their evidence would seem to demonstrate fairly conclusively that by about A.D. 175 infant baptism was well established across the Roman Empire, at least in the sense that some Christians were having their babies baptized. Such evidence would also suggest that the practice was very likely known in the early years of the second century. The *Apostolic Tradition*, Tertullian and Cyprian (and probably Origen too) all describe the "regular" baptism of infants rather than the emergency baptism of dying infants.

Another piece of evidence from the third century is found in the inscriptions on Christian tombstones.[19] Most of these are undated, but many are from the third century with no evidence that any of them are earlier. These clearly testify to two points. First, many babies and children were baptized. Secondly, many were baptized not at birth but at a later stage when they were in danger of death. No inscription says that a child was baptized as a baby and died at a later age. Emergency baptism was clearly common in the third century.[20]

---

[18]If the *Apostolic Tradition* is seen as a composite work, it might then reflect the practice of more than one region.

[19]Everett Ferguson, "Inscriptions and the Origin of Infant Baptism," *Journal of Theological Studies* 30 (1979): 37-46. Ferguson gives the text of many inscriptions (pp. 40-44).

[20]Why would it be seen as important that an infant should not die unbaptized? The belief that babies inherit not just a bias to sin but guilt does not appear to have been held by many in the second to fourth centuries. But John 3:5, "the favorite baptismal text of the second century," could easily be seen as implying that unbaptized infants would be excluded from heaven (ibid., p. 45).

Emergency baptism was not just for children. Inscriptions refer to adults, aged thirty-four and fifty-one for example, who were baptized shortly before death.

The evidence from the inscriptions reinforces the picture that we have already seen. Infant baptism is practiced, but not universally. Why were some not baptized as babies? We have no evidence, here or elsewhere, for any objection in principle to infant baptism. Elsewhere, evidence (as in Tertullian) reveals the fear of postbaptismal sin and the consequent postponement of baptism. This motive would equally explain the evidence of the inscriptions for the emergency baptism of mature adults as well as children.

Ferguson notes that "*all* of the inscriptions which mention a time of baptism place this near the time of death."[21] Deducing from this inscriptional evidence that infants were baptized *only* in case of emergency would be wrong. All adults whose baptism is dated were baptized shortly before death. One cannot deduce from this that adults were being baptized *only* at the point of death; rather that the date of the baptism is only mentioned on the inscription when it occurred shortly before death. The same is true for infants. Those infants whose baptism is not dated were probably baptized at an earlier stage. This is not an arbitrary conclusion, as the *Apostolic Tradition*, Tertullian and Cyprian all bear witness to the practice of infant baptism outside of the emergency context.

That the inscriptions only record baptismal dates in the case of emergency/deathbed baptism in no way proves that all baptisms were such, either for adults or for children. The inscriptions provide valuable evidence in that (like biographical evidence) they tell us what actually happened. They clearly prove that emergency baptisms happened for those of every age. They do not prove either that emergency baptism was the only form of baptism or that infants were baptized only in the case of emergency.

When is the first indisputable reference to infant baptism? We must

---

[21]Ibid., p. 44 (my emphasis). Only a small minority of inscriptions record the time of baptism.

turn to Tertullian and the *Apostolic Tradition*. Baptists sometimes make
much of the fact that no indisputable evidence for infant baptism dates
before A.D. 200, but this ignores an important point. When is the first
indisputable reference to the baptism at *any* age of someone from a
Christian home? Again, it is to Tertullian and the *Apostolic Tradition*
that we must turn. The earliest evidence concerning the baptism of
those raised as Christians is also evidence for the baptism of infants.
Thus the silence before the third century is not just a silence about
infant baptism; it is a silence about the church's policy and practice
regarding the baptism at *any* age of those raised as Christians.[22]

Tertullian indicates that although infant baptism may have been
practiced it was not the only form of initiation being proposed. Here,
as elsewhere, it would be easy to write Tertullian off as an inveterate
extremist. But in the third and fourth centuries many Christian families did follow the course that he recommended, not having their
children baptized. Tertullian's argument for the prudent delay of
baptism until the worst onslaughts of temptation were past struck a
chord and was followed in the fourth century by emperors and leading Christians. Neither in Tertullian nor in any other figure from
that time do we find any objection in principle to infant baptism nor
any denial of the claim that it was an apostolic practice. The only
controversy about infant baptism in the early church concerned why
it took place, rather than whether it should take place.[23]

Fourth and fifth centuries. What of the fourth and fifth centuries? A
number of facts are undisputed. Some babies were baptized and not
only at the point of death. No one objected in principle to infant
baptism. That does not mean that all Christians practiced it. David
Wright has shown that many of the leading Christians in the fourth
century were raised in Christian homes and baptized not as infants

---

[22]Regarding this silence, Jeremias, *Infant Baptism in the First Four Centuries,* p. 23, aptly
notes, "how seldom in the OT the circumcision of male infants is expressly mentioned."

[23]A point made by David F. Wright, "How Controversial Was the Development of Infant Baptism in the Early Church?" in *Church, Word, and Spirit,* ed. J. E. Bradley and
R. A. Muller (Grand Rapids: Eerdmans, 1987), pp. 50-51, 58-62, especially.

but as young adults.[24] None of these criticized their parents' policy.[25] This is significant data that demonstrates clearly that infant baptism was not regarded as normative in the fourth century, especially among elite godly families. But this data must not be mistaken for a statistical sample of fourth-century Christianity. This is a miniscule and unrepresentative sample and must not be allowed to obscure[26] the clear evidence elsewhere for the widespread (not necessarily majority) practice of infant baptism.[27]

After A.D. 300 the church fathers urged adults not to delay baptism, whether to postpone Christian commitment or for fear of post-baptismal sin. None of them proposed infant baptism as the only correct policy. Gregory Nazianzen's advice to Christian parents in his fortieth *Oration* is often quoted. Earlier in the oration he appears simply to commend the baptism of babies: "Have you an infant child? Do not let sin get any opportunity, but let him be sanctified from his childhood; from his very tenderest age let him be consecrated by the Spirit." Later and at greater length he offers a different recommendation. He recommends the immediate baptism of any babies in danger of death. For the rest, his advice is to wait until they are about three, "when they may be able to listen and to answer something about the sacrament; that, even though they do not perfectly understand it, yet at any rate they may know the outlines."

---

[24]David F. Wright, "At What Ages Were People Baptized in the Early Centuries?" *Studia Patristica* 30 (1997): 389-94. For the question of what, if anything, happened to babies instead of infant baptism, see David F. Wright, "Infant Dedication in the Early Church," in *Baptism, the New Testament and the Church,* ed. Stanley E. Porter and A. R. Cross (Sheffield, U.K.: Sheffield Academic Press, 1999), pp. 352-78.

[25]Wright, "At What Ages Were People Baptized," p. 393. Augustine criticized his mother for not allowing him to be baptized as a young boy (*Confessions* 1.11.17-18), but this was not for failure to secure him baptism as an *infant*.

[26]As for example in the statement that "the evidence is plentiful, with no instances to the contrary, that the baptizing of their newborn children had no place in the minds of even the most pious Christian parents during this period" (David F. Wright, "Monnica's Baptism, Augustine's Deferred Baptism, and Patricius," *Augustinian Studies* 29 [1998]: 10).

[27]The *Apostolic Constitutions* 6.15, of 370/80, urges the baptism of infants (PG 1:949-50; *ANF* 7:457). Jeremias, *Infant Baptism in the First Four Centuries*, pp. 92-97, gives other evidence starting from the middle of the fourth century.

This is the age when they begin to be responsible for their behavior and their reason is matured![28]

Three general points can be noted from the fourth century. First, there was a frank acceptance of a variety of policy. This clearly goes back to the third century, as is shown by the evidence of the inscriptions. Is there any reason for supposing that this variety does not go back further still? It is significant that we have no record in the third or fourth century of anyone objecting in principle to anyone else's policy, nor of anyone's policy being branded as a novelty. This fact strongly supports the theory that the diversity goes back a long way—perhaps even into the apostolic age.

Second, many fourth-century Christians did not have their babies baptized. Why not? One suggestion is that infant baptism was a novelty that had yet to become fully accepted, but we find no direct evidence for this. No one objected to the baptism of babies on the grounds that it was recent or unapostolic.[29] Others suggest that the baptism of believing converts was normative so that parents did not have infants baptized, waiting until the child came to a faith of his or her own.[30] Again no direct evidence for this is available, but it does cohere better with the known facts, that is, a variety of practice and infant baptism certainly not regarded as normative.

The biggest motivation for delaying baptism, and one for which we have clear direct evidence, was the fear of postbaptismal sin. There is no shortage of evidence from the fourth century of *adults* delaying baptism through fear of postbaptismal sin.[31] Apart from

---

[28]Gregory Nazianzen *Oration* 40.17, 28 (PG 36:379-82, 399-400; *NPNF*² 7:365, 370). For quotes from several of the church fathers on infant baptism, see <www.kathy schley.com/Early_Church_F/Infant_Baptisx.html>. I can confirm that when I was baptized at the age of three I did not "perfectly understand it."

[29]One could argue that the silence concerns not just this reason for not baptizing babies but the giving of any reason for it. But the silence suggests that whatever the reasons for not baptizing babies, these did not include any objection to it in principle, which would almost certainly have left some record.

[30]Paul Fiddes made this suggestion in a very helpful private communication (June 2002) in response to an earlier draft of this essay. He offers this as a second reason, in addition to the undoubted fear of postbaptismal sin.

[31]E.g., Chrysostom *Homily 1 on Acts*, from the very end of the century.

Tertullian less evidence is available for this motivation for the non-baptism of children, but it would be extraordinary for such fear to have caused adults to delay baptism without also motivating delay in the baptism of children. Tertullian argued that it was prudent to wait till youngsters had been through the years of teenage rebellion, sown their wild oats and were ready to settle down. This would be a good time to be baptized, thus effectively availing themselves of a once-only offer of amnesty, and to knuckle under to the rigors of the Christian life and church discipline.

Third, it is clear that fourth-century Christians had no objection *in principle* to infant baptism. They did, however, see the merits of coming to baptism at the point when its one-off benefits could be used to greatest effect. In the fifth-century West, infant baptism increasingly became the norm.[32] Various factors were at work, including an increasing emphasis on the doctrines of original sin and prevenient grace and the fear that babies dying unbaptized would go to hell. At this point for the first time infant baptism became expected of *all* children born to Christians.

When was the first objection *in principle* to infant baptism? The defence of an alternative to infant baptism goes back at least to Tertullian. Neither Tertullian nor anyone else in the early church objected in principle to infant baptism. They may have urged prudential considerations for the delay of baptism (not only for infants), but they did not suggest that the practice was unapostolic, illegitimate or invalid. Tertullian was not the sort of polemicist to pull punches like that had they had any plausibility. Augustine cited the practice of infant baptism as evidence for original sin, yet the Pelagians never questioned the validity of the practice. For such an objection in principle we have to wait until some small medieval

---

[32]Especially through the influence of Augustine in the context of the Pelagian controversy. But Pope Siricius could already in A.D. 385 urge the baptism of infants for fear that they might die unbaptized and so lose eternal life (*Epistola* 1.2.3 [PL 13:1134-35]; cf. *The Christian Faith in the Doctrinal Documents of the Catholic Church,* ed. Josef Neuner and Jacques Dupuis [London: Collins, 1983], p. 387).

sects[33] and the sixteenth-century Anabaptists.

If the practice were in fact unapostolic, it is surprising to say the least that none of those who had hesitations about it in the second to fourth centuries saw fit to draw attention to that fact. Had infant baptism been universally practiced in these centuries, its opponents today could plausibly argue that its unapostolic origins were for this reason suppressed. In fact infant baptism was far from universally practiced. No one would had any such motivation for concealing any suspicions that infant baptism was not an apostolic practice.

Second-century evidence. What about the second-century church? The direct evidence is much less clear. We have two accounts of baptism from that period. The *Didache*, or so-called *Teaching of the Twelve Apostles*, is probably from around the turn of the century, possibly even from the first century. It contains a few rules about how to conduct baptism but makes no mention of children.[34] Justin Martyr, writing from Rome about A.D. 150, gives a fuller description of a baptismal service, also without mentioning children.

This proves nothing, as the Jewish tractate *Gerim* gives regulations for proselyte baptism which are designed for adults only, yet elsewhere indicates that children were baptized.[35] The fact that no other sources from *this* time prove that babies were being baptized does not invalidate this comparison.[36] Also, Justin is explicitly describing the baptism of converts: "at our first birth we were born of

---

[33]H. Wheeler Robinson, *Baptist Principles* (London: Kingsgate, 1945), pp. 51, 62-64, draws attention to antisacramental protests against infant baptism in the twelfth-century West and to a Paulician document from ca. 800 titled *The Key of Truth* (pp. 58-62). For the text and translation of *The Key of Truth*, see Frederick C. Conybeare, *The Key of Truth, a Manual of the Paulician Church of Armenia* (Oxford: Clarendon Press, 1898).

[34]*Didache* 7. For a translation, see Cyril C. Richardson, *Early Christian Fathers*, LCC 1 (Philadelphia: Westminster Press, 1953), pp. 161-82.

[35]Joachim Jeremias, *Origins of Infant Baptism*, p. 39.

[36]Contra David F. Wright, "The Origins of Infant Baptism—Child Believer's Baptism?" *Scottish Journal of Theology* 40 (1987): 9-10. He speaks of Hippolytus as breaking the "ritual silence" concerning infant baptism (ibid., p. 10). This might give the impression that there were previous church orders that failed to mention it, which there were not. The regulations in the *Didache* are very brief and selective; Justin is writing an account for unbelievers, not giving liturgical directions.

necessity without our knowledge, from moist seed by the intercourse of our parents with each other, and were brought up in bad habits and wicked behaviour."[37] If this excludes Christian babies, it equally excludes adults raised in a Christian home. To deduce that either of these were not baptized is to read more into Justin than he says.

Sometime between A.D. 155 and 177 Polycarp, bishop of Smyrna, was martyred. At his trial he declared that he had served Christ for eighty-six years.[38] The eighty-six years takes us back at least to A.D. 91, possibly as far back as A.D. 69. Some in the past have claimed, rather optimistically, that this proves infant baptism. The most that can be said is that the reference is probably to the years since his baptism and that it is likely that he was still a child when baptized.

The most significant testimony from the second century comes from Irenaeus, who grew up in Asia Minor (modern Turkey) but was writing from Lyon in the early 180s. In the context of teaching that Christ sanctified every stage of life, he writes: "For [Christ] came to save all through means of himself—all, I say, who through him are born again to God—infants, small children, youngsters, youths and old folk."[39] Given his usage elsewhere, "born again to God" must refer to baptism.[40] Since infants are distinguished from small children and youngsters, the reference must be to those too young to speak. It is hard to see what Irenaeus can mean if infant baptism is not in mind.

The only substantial evidence for infant baptism from the second century is Irenaeus's statement, although the instructions in the *Apostolic Tradition* may go back to the middle of that century. As has been argued above, the evidence *for* the second century is not limited

[37]*First Apology* 61 (ACW 56:66-67. Cf. PG 6:419-22; *ANF* 1:183).

[38]*Martyrdom of Polycarp* 9. For translation see <mb-soft.com/believe/txv/polycar2.htm> or <www.ccel.org/ccel/schaff/anf01.toc.html>. See printed text in Greek and English in *The Martyrdom of Polycarp,* trans. Kirsopp Lake (Whitefish, Mont.: Kessinger Publishing, 2005).

[39]*Against Heresies* 2.22.4 (*ANF* 1:391 [modified]). Cf. PG 7:784; SC 294:220-21).

[40]*Against Heresies* 1.21.1, 3.17.1, 5.15.3. Cf. SC 293:287. Aland, *Did the Early Church Baptize Infants?* pp. 58-59, correctly notes Jeremias's failure to consider the wider context, but fails to suggest an alternative meaning for this particular statement.

to evidence *from* the second century. Given the fact of tradition, one can draw conclusions from the statements of Tertullian and Origen in the third century about what was happening in the previous century. Finally, we cannot assume one uniform policy in all branches of the church. Practices may well have varied by region and according to individual choice.

First-century evidence. If the second-century evidence is weak, for the first century we are reduced to hints. Most explicit are the household or family baptisms of Acts 16:15, 33 and 1 Corinthians 1:16. It seems clear that this was the baptism not just of several individuals but of a family unit. Did this include babies? It is hard to be certain. It is unlikely, but not impossible, that none of these families included babies. Other household passages can be taken as pointing the other way. Acts 18:8 refers to a whole family believing. Cornelius is told that it is through a message that his household will be saved (Acts 11:14). The passage implies those who heard the message received the Spirit and then were baptized (Acts 10:44-48).

Some scholars say that just as these passages must exclude babies, so also the reference to family baptisms cannot include infants. Others have suggested that the concept of the family as a unit means that babies could be referred to as believers—just as people have no problem referring to Jewish or Hindu babies. Third-century epitaphs on some of the tombs of babies refer to them as believing on the grounds that they were baptized.[41] The most natural reading of the references to household baptism, especially in the context of the Old Testament background, is that children were included. But this falls short of definite proof.

Jewish proselyte baptism was given to the whole family, including the youngest children. But it was not given to children subsequently born into the family. It has been suggested, on the basis of 1 Corinthians 7:14, that this might mean that babies were baptized when a family converted but that future children were not baptized at all.[42]

[41]Ferguson, "Inscriptions," p. 40.
[42]This passage is discussed by Wright, "Origins of Infant Baptism," pp. 14-17, who men-

To suggest that such were never baptized is an interesting theoretical interpretation of that verse, but does not square with history.

Paul addressed his readers on the assumption that they were all baptized, while the suggested policy would mean that by that time Rome, for example, would have had young adult Christians who had not been and would never be baptized. The sources offer no evidence that any group of people were ever exempted from the need to be baptized. Such a policy would make nonsense of the New Testament theology of baptism. We must not discount the possibility that, while existing children were baptized with their parents (as with proselyte baptism), subsequent children were baptized only at a later stage.[43] If this were so, we would have a variety of practice already in New Testament times. This would account for the non-dogmatic approach taken in the following three centuries.

Mark 10:13-16 has long been cited as a proof of infant baptism. Jesus urges the disciples to let the children come to him. They are not to be hindered, a term that already in the New Testament (Mt 3:14; Acts 8:36; 10:47; 11:17), as well as later, refers to obstacles to receiving baptism. Jesus lays hands on the children. Tertullian records the Greek term's reference to infant baptism, but it is unlikely to have that meaning in Mark. The only other surviving patristic source before Augustine to associate the text with infant baptism is the Syrian *Apostolic Constitutions* of A.D. 370/80.[44]

The seismological scenarios. So far we have looked for direct evidence for or against infant baptism. It is widely recognized that the surviving evidence does not enable a clear answer to be given for any time period prior to about A.D. 175. Our seismological approach pro-

---

tions Jeremias's earlier suggestion (Jeremias, *Infant Baptism in the First Four Centuries,* pp. 47-48). Wright correctly argues that the holiness of the children cannot have been based on their baptism, but goes too far in deducing that they therefore cannot have been baptized (ibid., pp. 14-15). Might their baptism not have been based on their "holiness"?

[43]Wright, "Origins of Infant Baptism," pp. 18, 22, discusses this possibility.

[44]For the history of the use of this text see David Wright, "Out, In, Out: Jesus' Blessing of the Children and Infant Baptism," in *Dimensions of Baptism,* ed. S. E. Porter and A. R. Cross (London: Sheffield Academic Press, 2002), pp. 188-206.

vides an alternative way to answer the question. In the third and
fourth centuries, the earliest period for which we have clear evidence, church practices show a variety. Christian children were baptized at every conceivable age. How can we account for this variety?
We may construct three reasonable scenarios for the earliest apostolic
church: (1) they did not baptize Christian babies, (2) they did baptize
Christian babies, or (3) already at this stage variety prevailed among
the churches.

Which of these three scenarios is the most plausible, given the
evidence? Consider the first scenario: that infants were not baptized.
How is the later variety to be explained? Perhaps it began with emergency baptism of sick children, and this led on to more regular infant
baptism.[45] What is the evidence for this? On the one hand the inscriptions offer evidence for the emergency baptism of small children. On the other hand the surviving Christian literature from the
first five centuries gives no hint anywhere that anyone objected *in
principle* to infant baptism, that anyone considered it improper, irregular or invalid. If it were a postapostolic innovation, this silence
is remarkable. The emergency baptism of dying infants implies an
acceptance in principle that baptizing infants is not wrong. If this
were in defiance of apostolic practice, it is hard to believe that no
single trace of protest would have survived—especially when no
shortage of Christians chose not to baptize their children while others recommended delay in baptism.

Tertullian sought to discourage infant baptism, but failed to use
what would have been his most powerful argument—the claim that
it was unapostolic. No single piece of evidence from the first two
centuries portrays a child brought up as a Christian but baptized at a
later age. If the problem with infant baptism is *inconclusive* evidence
that it happened in the first 150 years of the church, the problem
with the alternative theory is *total lack* of evidence. Admittedly the
New Testament evidence for the baptism of infants is inconclusive,

[45]As is argued by Ferguson, "Inscriptions," pp. 44-46.

but at least some passages may be plausibly interpreted as implying that infants were baptized—such as Acts 16:33. By contrast no New Testament evidence at all points to the later baptism of Christian children. We have no record of such a baptism and no hint in the epistles that such children should be seeking baptism.

Consider now the second scenario: that the earliest church did in fact baptize babies. While no unequivocal proof that this did happen remains, we do possess what can quite plausibly be seen as evidence of infant baptism at this time. Whole households were baptized, and these incidents can at least plausibly be seen as examples of infant baptism. In the New Testament epistles the instruction given to the churches includes instruction to children (Eph 6:1-4; Col 3:20). These children are not encouraged or instructed to be baptized, nor are their parents instructed to work to that end. Instead the children are addressed as Christians, which fits best with the theory that they are baptized.

If the earliest practice was the baptism of infants, how is it that in later centuries not all Christian babies were baptized? Tertullian urges just such a change on the ground of his fear of postbaptismal sin. Given the attitude of the second-century church to postbaptismal sin, seen in *The Shepherd* of Hermas for example, it is plausible that the delay in baptism began in the second century. In other words if babies were baptized in the earliest church we find no difficulty in accounting for the later variation in practice. Parents who delayed the baptism of their babies did not do so because of any objection in principle to infant baptism but for prudential reasons, because of the fear of postbaptismal sin. The parents would of course wish to have those children baptized should they fall ill and be in danger of death. Thus this theory fully explains the existence of emergency baptism of children. Against this theory remains the fact that Tertullian and others who urged delay in baptism were never accused of departing from the New Testament or from apostolic tradition.

We take a look at the final scenario: variety of practice in the apostolic church. This is the most likely, based on the later evidence and using our seismological approach.[46] After all, the earliest *unequivocal* evidence for the initiation of Christian children comes from a time (early third century) when we know that there was variety of practice. What could have caused the variety? We can point to a number of options. We have already proposed the difference between babies born before and after their parents' baptism. Another option would be different policies for Jews, who circumcised their children, and Gentiles who did not. It is also possible that variety was introduced as the church spread into different places.

The evidence from the New Testament that babies were baptized is impressive, though not conclusive. The evidence that *all* Christian babies were baptized is, of course, much weaker. While the New Testament offers no positive evidence for such a variety of practice, the later existence of a variety which is widespread, enduring and unchallenged leads us as seismologists to enquire about its origins and to ask whether it might not go back to the apostolic church.

Such a hypothesis would explain the fact that we have no evidence for any objection in principle against either the baptism or the nonbaptism of babies. This hypothesis finds support by the fact that as far back as we have unequivocal evidence of how Christian children were initiated (early third century) we find variety. No evidence can be presented against the existence of such variety in the first and second centuries.

Seismological conclusions. So what conclusion do we reach as twenty-first-century seismologists, drawing on the reports of witnesses from closer to the epicenter of the earthquake? Our evidence has not been confined to those witnesses residing at the epicenter itself but has

---

[46]David F. Wright, "George Cassander and the Appeal to the Fathers in Sixteenth-Century Debates About Infant Baptism," in *Auctoritas Patrum. Contributions on the Reception of the Church Fathers in the 15th and 16th Century,* ed. L. Grane, A. Schindler, M. Wriedt (Mainz: Philipp von Zabern, 1993), p. 267, observes that "differences of category of infants, of circumstances and even of region alone make sense of the evidence." (He also interestingly shows that the Anabaptist Menno Simons accepted that infant baptism took place in the apostolic age, though regarding it as an abuse [p. 264].) Jeremias, *Infant Baptism in the First Four Centuries,* pp. 43-44, also postulates such variation.

also been drawn from nearby witnesses who witnessed the more immediate aftereffects. This evidence leads to a number of conclusions.

The meager evidence from the first two centuries is consistent with the practice of infant baptism but does not demand it. The evidence from the third and fourth centuries unambiguously reveals a diversity in practice where the initiation of Christian children is concerned. A total lack of evidence appears in the first four centuries of any objection *in principle* to either the baptism or the nonbaptism of babies. Given this evidence, what is most likely to have occurred in the apostolic church? That the practice of infant baptism was unknown seems to me to be the least likely hypothesis. That it was practiced seems very likely. That it was *universally* practiced is much less likely given the freedom that later Christians felt not to baptize their children.

THEOLOGICAL ISSUES
Two strategies. Discussions of infant baptism often become polarized. Should a child be baptized as a baby or at some later stage when he or she comes to their own personal faith? Put this way, we have a choice between two clear alternatives. In fact, far more common ground exists between the two sides than is often recognized. Many churches observe some sort of dedication ceremony after the birth of the child. This is followed by a period of Christian nurture within the church over a period of many years. If all goes well, it concludes with the grown-up child making a personal public confession of faith in baptism. In other churches the newborn baby is baptized. This is followed by a period of Christian nurture within the church over a period of many years. If all goes well, it concludes with the grown-up child making a personal public confession of faith in an adult ceremony which may or may not be called confirmation.

As regards the timing of baptism, these two strategies are diametrically opposed. Apart from that, they are remarkably similar. That is why Baptists and paedobaptists are able to cooperate happily together in so many areas without serious tension. In Britain teams work with children at the "Spring Harvest" family week events without anyone knowing (or caring) whether or not the children attending have been baptized. Those who offer to help in this work are not asked whether they are Baptist or paedobaptist. Why not? Is this a heroic determination to cooperate together despite serious differences? Or is it because the question both seems and is all but totally irrelevant to what is taking place? The program of Christian nurture, that which takes place between the first and second "rite," is not significantly different for baptized and unbaptized children. That is why those who publish Bible-reading notes for children do not provide separate sets for those who have/have not been baptized.

It is reasonable to regard both of the strategies outlined above as different, but legitimate, adaptations of the converts' baptism of Acts to the changed situation of the nurture of children in a Christian home. Both demand a program of Christian nurture which, in the last resort, is more important than any of the ceremonies. The important point to remember here and at every stage is that the question is not just about when to administer baptism. To discuss it in those terms both polarizes unnecessarily and also distorts the issue. It must always be remembered that for those raised in a Christian home, baptism, whether as an infant or an adult, is not an isolated event but simply one stage in a lengthy process. To lose this perspective makes any resolution of the issue much harder, and effectively impossible. For example, attempts to defend infant baptism as itself complete initiation (rather than the beginning of a process of initiation) are misguided.

But how feasible is it to expect churches to treat the two strategies as "equivalent alternatives"?[47] Many will regard this as hopelessly idealistic, but that is not so. In the first place, throughout the early church whenever we have clear evidence, the children of Christian families were being baptized at every conceivable age. Indeed, no

---

[47]The phrase comes from the agreed statement *Baptism, Eucharist and Ministry* (Geneva: World Council of Churches, 1982), p. 5 (Baptism section, commentary on 3.12).

evidence remains from the early church that the situation was ever
different nor that anyone ever denied the legitimacy of such variety,
though each course had its strong advocates.[48]

Second, many, if not most, paedobaptist churches today accept the
fact that not all Christian parents wish to have their children baptized. The churches make provision for alternative ceremonies such
as dedication or blessing. Barth and Moltmann, two hugely significant theologians from the twentieth-century European Reformed
churches, both opposed the practice of infant baptism. Calls for an
alternative approach have even come from within the Roman Catholic Church.[49]

Most paedobaptist denominations are able to accommodate the
fact that some of their members will prefer not to baptize their
children but to bring them up in the hope that they will seek believers' baptism at a later age. It is harder for Baptists to come to
terms with this as many of them still regard infant baptism as no
baptism at all, or at best highly irregular. While the practice of
believers' baptism for the children of Christian homes was widespread in the early church, the Baptist rejection of infant baptism
was totally unknown.

Finally, the dual practice approach has not been unknown in recent centuries. In seventeenth-century England a group of Baptist
churches began to accept either practice, and the church at Bedford,
now named after Bunyan, has maintained this approach down to the
present day.[50]

The silence of the Bible. A famous tract reads on the outside, "What
the Bible teaches about infant baptism." When the tract is opened,
the inside pages turn out to be empty! This is a clever but misleading

[48]I am thinking especially of Tertullian and Pope Siricius urging the nonbaptism and
baptism of infants respectively.

[49]See, e.g., Phillippe Béguerie and Claude Duchesneau, *How to Understand the Sacraments*
(London: SCM Press, 1991), pp. 121-22, although they are overly optimistic in claiming that "the church has always known this diversity of positions."

[50]Meic Pearse, *The Great Restoration: The Religious Radicals of the 16th and 17th Centuries*
(Carlisle, U.K.: Paternoster, 1998), pp. 212-13.

apologetic ploy. More honestly, the outside of the tract should read, "What the New Testament teaches about the initiation of children brought up in a Christian home." No explicit answer to this question appears in the New Testament, though some material (such as the family baptisms) can be interpreted as supporting one side or the other. What should we make of this silence in the New Testament? It could so easily have been resolved. All that was needed was the addition of a brief phrase to Acts 16:33. To "he and all his family were baptized," Luke could have added, "babies, children and adults," or "all who were old enough to answer for themselves," or "all who had reached adulthood," or some such clause. But it is not there. Why not?

Does not acceptance of the authority of Scripture mean respecting the silences of Scripture as well as its positive statements? The silences are there to leave the church liberty to vary its practice to suit different circumstances. They sanction the variety of practice that we see in the early church.

The aforementioned tract presumes that this question is to be answered by reference to the New Testament alone. Others (no doubt including Sinclair Ferguson in this volume) would want to place some emphasis on the teaching of the Old Testament, especially on the fact that infants were circumcised. The question of the relation between the Testaments is important and determines people's attitudes on a variety of issues, such as the significance of the sabbath law, pacifism and the possibility of a state church. Usually it functions as an *unacknowledged* presupposition, with the result that people are unable to agree because they are arguing from different premises.

In fact all Christians would agree that both an element of continuity (at the very least, they are both about the same God) and an element of discontinuity (Christians no longer offer animal sacrifices, for example) exists between the Testaments. The difference comes in the relative proportions of continuity and discontinuity. In the present context, those emphasizing the continuity between the

Testaments are likely to stress the *one* covenant of grace, while those emphasizing the discontinuity are more likely to stress the novelty of the *new* covenant. Baptists and paedobaptists are each able to appeal to different aspects of biblical theology. Do we have to rule out one of these appeals as illegitimate, or can we accept the ensuing variety as legitimate diversity—as did the Christians of the third and fourth centuries, and probably also those of the first and second centuries?

The role of diversity. In some practical issues the individual must make a choice, but the church can benefit from diversity. An individual cannot at the same time be both married and single. It is important for the church both that the majority of Christians marry and form Christian families and that a minority remain celibate, like Jesus and Paul, and bear witness to the transcendent values of the kingdom. Again, no individual can both fight and be a pacifist, yet both witness to important aspects of truth. A church composed solely of pacifists would be dangerously out of touch with society. Yet a church all of whose members were prepared to fight would have lost an important strand of the gospel.

A related issue is the value of the study of theology both in the public arena, in secular universities, and in the confessional setting of the seminary. Each has its complementary strengths and weaknesses. The church would suffer a loss if either ceased to exist. In short, in some practical areas no one policy can bear witness to the fullness of truth, where different Christians may have contradictory callings and yet together bear witness to the full range of God's truth.

So also with this subject. Any one Christian baby is either baptized or is not, but it is valuable for the church that both policies are followed. Paedobaptists bear witness against the individualism of the postmodern age and point to God's dealings with families. Infant baptism bears witness to God's prevenient grace, to his work in and through the community. Baptists by contrast bear witness against the scourge of nominal Christianity and remind us that in the strict sense God has no grandchildren. Believers' baptism bears witness against the dangers of a secondhand faith, whereas infant baptism can lead those

raised in Christian homes to imagine that they are already Christians
and do not need to make a personal response of faith.

Each policy leads to anomalies. Infant baptism means the baptism
of some who will grow up to be unbelievers. This has become especially scandalous because of the practice of indiscriminate infant
baptism, with the result that in Europe tens of millions are baptized
but have hardly ever set foot in a church. The problem is far less
acute if infant baptism is restricted to those who are going to receive
a Christian upbringing, yet even with such the church has no guarantee that they will in due course come to a living personal faith.

This problem is not confined to paedobaptists. Unfortunately no
shortage exists of people who have been baptized as believers but
have subsequently abandoned their faith. Also, the Baptist model
creates the anomaly of children who have a living faith but are unbaptized, a situation foreign to the New Testament concept of converts' baptism. The situation is less acute for those who genuinely
hold to believers' baptism (being ready to baptize four-year-old believers, for example) than for those who believe only in adult believers' baptism (being unwilling to baptize believers under twelve years
old, or whatever other age has been decreed).

Status of Christian children. Are the children of Christians to be
viewed as Christians or as pagans? Sometimes the question is posed
in this stark way, but the truth of the matter is not so simple. In practice Christians, even Baptists, do not treat their children as pagans.
They take their children to church. They teach them to pray—and
teach them to pray specifically Christian prayers. When a nine-year-
old comes back from school uttering blasphemous expletives, parents
inform the child that such talk is not acceptable in this household.

Again, in practice evangelical Christians at least do not treat their
little children as fully fledged Christians. However high their view
of infant baptism (even if, like Luther or Wesley, they believe in
baptismal regeneration), they recognize that the child will need to
come to a personal commitment as he or she grows up. As society
becomes more secular, Christendom becomes more and more a thing

of the past and purely nominal Christianity becomes rarer, Christians across the spectrum increasingly recognize this truth. Catholic Christians may once have emphasized that infants become Christians at baptism. Today they increasingly acknowledge the need for this to become "interiorized" as a personal decision if the child is going to continue to be a practicing Christian. What was once very much an evangelical distinctive (the need for conversion) is becoming much more widely acknowledged.

The picture has two sides. Just as we talk of Jewish, Muslim and Hindu children, so we can also talk of Christian children—those being nurtured in a Christian home. In the modern secular world parents who presume upon this and imagine that their children are "home and dry" are liable to have a rude awakening. Those who baptize their children bear witness to one side of the picture; those who do not baptize them bear witness to the other. It is healthy that both practices take place. Instead of attacking those who pursue the other strategy, we should be ready to learn from them that to which our own strategy is liable to blind us.

The individual and the corporate. Significantly the Baptist view both emerged and grew in popularity at the same time as the rise of modern Western individualism. The Baptist model is of the baptism of independent, freestanding, autonomous individuals. How should this be assessed? Is the Baptist view a skillful and legitimate contextualization of the gospel into modern Western society? Or is it an accommodation of the gospel which betrays it to modern Western culture? The trouble is that one person's contextualization can be another person's accommodation! It would be possible to argue consistently that the early church did baptize infants, that universal infant baptism was a legitimate policy during the period of Christendom when children were reared in a Christian environment but that in the climate of today's postmodern and individualistic culture the best policy is not to baptize infants.

Baptists will, of course, protest that the gospel, not modern individualism, urges the individual to put loyalty to God and Christ above loyalty to the family (e.g., Mt 10:35-37, 12:46-50). This is true, but similar demands are found in the Old Testament when infants were circumcised. It remains true that the understanding of these passages to exclude infant baptism came with the rise of individualism.

Paedobaptists lay greater stress on the corporate side of salvation. They would point to the way in which God, in the Old Testament, deals not just with individuals but with families, as with Noah and, supremely, Abraham. Old Testament faith and religion was a family and community matter, not just an individual matter. They would see the household baptisms of Acts as being the baptism of a family unit, not just of a collection of individuals all of whom happened to believe.

This point would remain true even if it happened that no children were present. Infant baptism has also, historically, been linked with the doctrine of original sin—either doctrine offering support to the other as the need arose! The doctrine of original sin implies that sin is not purely individual, that we experience such a thing as the corporate sin of the human race. Babies are not born totally innocent. This used to provide a compelling motivation for infant baptism when it was feared that infants dying unbaptized would be lost. Indeed Baptists have argued that infant baptism arose because of a misguided fear of infant damnation. Today, however, the majority of Christians would not accept that dying unbaptized excluded babies from salvation.

Where there may be a practical difference between the two strategies is in the status of children in the church. At what age can children receive God's grace and respond to it? (There are similar issues with the status of the mentally handicapped.) Is faith something properly possible only for adults, or can a little child truly believe? Is conversion the mature decision of an autonomous adult, or is it possible for children to convert? Should we think in terms of a family church or an adult church?

If one accepts that both ways (the paedobaptist way and the Baptist way) are legitimate, the question of the nature of the church becomes crucial.

On the paedobaptist model children are regarded as part of the church from the beginning and may in principle be admitted to communion at any stage. On the Baptist model children remain unbaptized until they reach a mature adult age. Unless one is going to make nonsense of the sacraments, such children should not receive communion. Parents deciding whether or not to baptize young children should perhaps ask themselves the following question: When their child has real faith but is too young to make the adult step which marks the end of the process of initiation, should that child be accepted as a member of the church and receive communion? If the answer is yes, infant baptism is the logical conclusion. If the answer is no, the Baptist way is the logical conclusion.

CONCLUSION

The New Testament practice of baptism was converts' baptism, the immediate baptism of those who come to faith as part of their initial response to the gospel. This needs to be modified for children born into a Christian home, either into infant baptism or into baptism at a later date. The New Testament evidence for how such children were treated is not unambiguous. Both approaches can be defended on biblical grounds. No grounds exist for insisting on one to the exclusion of the other. This policy of accepting diversity is the *only* policy for which the first four centuries of the church provide any clear evidence.

BELIEVERS' BAPTISM RESPONSE

Bruce A. Ware

TONY LANE'S CHAPTER WAS VERY INTERESTING and also quite intriguing. Not only was the reader assured from the very opening sentence that this chapter would describe the "correct view" (tongue only partly in cheek, I suspect), but it also became clear early on that for one to adopt this view as correct, one must deny that the Bible actually teaches a normative and specific position on the practice of baptism, however that is understood.

One area where Professor Ferguson and I surely will agree is this: Professor Lane's view simply cannot be correct, as he claims. Even if Professor Ferguson and I may never agree on just what the normative and specific teaching of the New Testament is regarding the practice of baptism, it is a step even further to conclude that there is no such normative teaching to be understood and practiced. This, it seems to me, is the main problem with Lane's position: it denies that the Bible actually specifies one practice as correct when most Christians have read the Bible as indicating that some one practice is correct, despite their differences on just what that one correct practice is.

I appreciate the candor of the discussion Lane offers early in his chapter on the New Testament evidence for believers' baptism. As he indicates, in at least fourteen passages some or all of the following elements occur together marking conversion: repentance, faith, baptism and reception of the Holy Spirit. He is correct to observe that as one examines these texts, and especially as one considers every instance of the practice of baptism, that believers' baptism is the unbroken and uniform practice in the New Testament. So clear is this evidence that he writes, "Surely it is abundantly clear that the practice of the apostles as recorded in Acts was believers' baptism, the baptism of those who had come to faith and repentance, the position taken by Baptists today" (pp. 142-43). Perhaps the reader will pardon this Baptist's enthusiasm in exclaiming, "If only Professor Lane had seen the wisdom of staying with the practice of the apostles!" Of course he has reasons for concluding otherwise. Mr. Lane's acknowledgment does seem to weigh heavily in favor of the credobaptist position, should one conclude that a normative doctrine of the nature and practice of baptism is taught in the New Testament.

Given this preliminary conclusion from Professor Lane that favors the Baptist position, one cannot help but puzzle over his subsequent wandering off and away from the Baptist trail, as one sees it in the New Testament. What seem to be the main factors leading to this departure? First, Lane is convinced (and gives credit partially to Beasley-Murray) that baptism in the New Testament is not so much of believers per se, but of converts. In response, surely even today we realize that when we baptize "believers" we do so trusting that they truly have believed in Christ, although all we can see, as it were, is that they have professed belief in Christ and so are converts to the Christian faith. The New Testament does not speak this way, even though it likewise is aware of the problem at times of false profession of faith (e.g., 1 Cor 15:2; Tit 1:16). The New Testament, rather, speaks of one (or those) who "believed" and were "baptized." Acts 8:12-13 will suffice as an example: "But when they *believed* Philip as he preached good news about the kingdom of God and the name of Jesus Christ, they were *baptized*, both men and women. Even Simon himself *believed*, and after being *baptized* he continued with Philip. And seeing signs and great miracles performed, he was amazed" (emphasis added). While one might ask, "How can we be sure these truly are believers and not merely outward converts?" the New Testament, while understanding this possibility and reality, also understands that the purpose of baptism is to signify the spiritual reality that transpires by faith. Hence it is always "believers" and not "converts" who are said to be baptized.

Second, how then does Lane include infants in the baptism of the early church? Here, his "seismological" approach seems to be key to his position that the likelihood of infant baptism, along with believers' baptism, can be seen early in the church from what was more widely reported later. As he states in one place, "In the third and fourth centuries, the earliest period for which we have clear evidence, there was variety in practice. Christian children were baptized at every conceivable age" (pp. 159-60). He argues that since this variety can be seen in later centuries, it stands to reason that this same variety must have been practiced earlier also. That is, given the later variety of practice, we can infer also an earlier variety of practice. This should indicate to us today the flexibility with which the church should approach the question of baptism.

Imagine where we would be in the church if we applied the same kind of seismological approach to other areas of Christian faith and practice. If it is the case that variety in belief and practice indicates that the church should adopt a flexible stance toward these areas on which we exhibit such variety, what areas of Christian faith or practice would be left definite? One can appreciate the greater difficulty that such variety in Christian belief and practice creates in determining convictions and practices for oneself or within a believing community, but certainly it seems unwarranted, in principle, to tend toward flexibility today if one can demonstrate variety in the past. Does not the question of what the Bible teaches on this or any subject become paramount over any historical record, including a record of variety of belief and practice?

Continuing this last question, it seems to me that Lane's own position argues largely from this historical record while leaving behind the fine biblical study that began his chapter. Perhaps I regret his

later move because the early pages of his chapter so clearly advance a
Baptist understanding. More importantly, Lane's position seems to
depend largely not on the teaching of Scripture but on the historical
record that he has detected, using the seismological approach he describes at some length. In the end, and with the Reformers, we must
stand with *sola Scriptura* as the only final and only absolutely authoritative source for our belief and practice as Christians. If the Bible
presents a doctrine of baptism along with a corresponding practice of
baptism expressive of this doctrine, then the historical record must
take its rightful secondary place. Since I am convinced that the Bible
in fact presents such a doctrine and practice of baptism, Lane's "no
position" position (or perhaps "any position" position) simply cannot
be correct, despite his hopeful claim.

One final comment seems appropriate. Lane's appeal to both
paedo- and credobaptists to consider coming together, accepting
each other's practice of baptism in a unified church, strikes me as
fully unrealistic. Whether one considers Lane's proposal to be something of a utopian vision of a new ecumenism or more akin to a call
to depart from deeply held and cherished convictions, the simple fact
is that firm believers on all sides of this issue would find themselves
compromised should they consider seriously adopting Lane's approach. I recall a struggle I had with this very question early in my
adult life and ministry. During a portion of my doctoral studies at
Fuller Seminary in Pasadena, California, my wife and I attended a
very fine and vibrant evangelical church that was part of the Evangelical Covenant denomination. So fond was I of this church and
many of its leaders that I explored the possibility of becoming part of
the denomination. My dreams however were almost immediately
dashed when I learned from a denominational official that those
ordained in the Evangelical Covenant would need to be open to
baptizing either infants or believers in any Covenant church they
served, depending on the desires of parents within one's congregation. What became immediately clear to me was this: this so-called
inclusive view of baptism in fact included only those who held no

particular view of baptism, while it excluded any and all of those
who had convictions that the Bible taught a normative doctrine and
practice of New Testament baptism. Being this as it is, I cannot but
conclude that even if Professor Lane's view were to be correct
(though I am convinced it is not), there simply is no practical way it
could become widely held and practiced among Bible-believing
churches. For all of the appeal it may have to some, I do not believe
it to be a position that comports either with Scripture's clear teaching or with reason, which would seem, contrary to Lane's hopes and
longings, to demonstrate that it lacks practical viability.

INFANT BAPTISM RESPONSE

Sinclair B. Ferguson

PROFESSOR TONY LANE HAS PROVIDED a lucid and engaging exposition of his dual-practice view of baptism, marked by a happy mixture of clarity of historical survey with self-deprecating humor. Both theology and baptism are serious matters, but theologians should not take their own significance as seriously as they do their theology. Professor Lane is convinced of the rightness of his view of baptism (as a theologian should be). But readers will happily recognize that anyone converted to believers' baptism by the *Commentary on Romans* of (I assume) the paedobaptists Sanday and Headlam,[1] only to be unconverted from it by the credobaptist George Beasley-Murray[2] surely has the happy grace of not taking himself too seriously!

DIVERSITY IS NOT DUAL PRACTICE

Dual practice has dual forms. Evangelical paedobaptists today often experience church life that is not too dissimilar from Tony Lane's dual practice view. Presbyterians (the only kind of Christian I have ever been, but doubtless the same would apply to Congregationalists, Episcopalians, even some Christian Brethren) baptize those who

---

[1]William Sanday and Arthur C. Headlam, *Romans*, International Critical Commentary (Edinburgh: T & T Clark, 1895).
[2]G. R. Beasley-Murray, *Baptism in the New Testament* (London: Macmillan, 1962).

have come to faith in Christ ("converts' baptism") and (if there are any) their children ("infant baptism"). Speaking personally as a paedobaptist, this is one of the great joys of twenty-first-century pastoral ministry.

But this is not the diversity for which Dr. Lane argues. If I understand him right, the great *desideratum* is for a dual practice (which he thinks may be original in the church) in which both credo- and paedobaptist practices (and therefore presumably theologies) exist within the same congregation, and on mutually valid footing. Thus, in contrast to paedobaptist theology and practice, the *sufficient* doctrinal grounds for baptizing infants may not be regarded as *necessary* grounds. The implication appears to be that the choice is left in the hands of . . . whom?

Approach to the evidence from antiquity. What Professor Lane calls his "seismological approach" to the issue is suggestive of an interesting and fruitful analogy. It may also be a useful model for other discussions of controverted areas in the history of theology. It provides an intelligent and healthy approach to the evidence for baptism in the early centuries of the church. Too much has been made, in my own view, of the appeal to antiquity without taking cognizance of the specific context and the specific form of the arguments used in patristic discussions of baptism. Dr. Lane judiciously notes the importance of theological tactics here. Particularly noteworthy in my own view is the correlation of baptism and forgiveness with the debated question of whether postbaptismal sin is forgivable. This is an altogether different discussion from debate over the theological legitimacy of infant baptism per se. The historical evidence is misread if it is assumed that these debates were simply an early form of later credo- and paedobaptist disagreements.

The importance of context. I appreciate and share Professor Lane's reserve in reading too much into emergency baptism and in particular the extant inscriptions on the tombs of those who have died in childhood. His conclusions seem to me to be a more reliable handling of the evidence than those which others have drawn. The close association of baptism and salvation/forgiveness of sins, and the lack of confidence in the forgiveness of postbaptismal sin that provided the impetus for postponing baptism is, in my own view, both a sufficient and a more likely explanation of why parents would be especially anxious to note that their child had been baptized prior to death.

Following this line of thought beyond Dr. Lane's conclusion, convinced third-century "credobaptist" parents would surely no more lay aside their convictions even in the face of death than would twenty-first-century ones. That parents brought their children for baptism should therefore not be thought of as a knee-jerk reaction to mortal sickness—as though better judgment would have dictated otherwise. Here again the context of the early debates and the nature of the reasoning differs considerably from contemporary credobaptist-paedobaptist polemics.

Significant silence. Coherent interpretation of historically situated theological reasoning must take account not only of what is said, but also of what is *not* said. Again Professor Lane illustrates this principle. He is surely right to note that the context of the early church's discussions of baptism was one in which authoritative tradition, traced back to the apostles, carried great weight. The absence (in arguments for not baptizing infants) of an appeal *ad fontes,* as it were, is telling. For this underlines that the grounds of the argument over infant baptism in antiquity differ from those of the modern period. Reaching *apparently similar practical conclusions* (the delay of baptism) by no means indicates *the same theological rationale.* That the early church had no objection to the theological principles grounding the baptism of infants is an important observation, albeit too often overlooked.

A major conclusion. Professor Lane offers us three possible conclusions from the evidence of the first three centuries. In the earliest (apostolic?) churches:

1. Infants were not baptized; or,
2. Infants were baptized; or,
3. Some infants were baptized, while others were not.

He concludes that exclusive credobaptism is least likely to have been the practice of the apostles. The practice of infant baptism in the church seems likely, but its universal practice less so. In all likelihood, therefore, the diversity of practice in the later church may well reflect the practice of the first century.

Questions about diversity. Here it is necessary to ask exactly what kind of "diversity" is in view here. Specifically what would be required to justify the "dual practice" for which Professor Lane argues? Would it not need to be the practice of baptizing converts *and* the baptism of their children and also the nonbaptism of their children—that is, each of these positions would stand on equal footing within the church(es)?

Furthermore would this diversity of baptismal practice not also need to be evident within a single congregation (and/or area) to indicate clearly that the church endorsed a genuinely tolerated diversity in practice and theology? In addition, to claim this to be an authoritative practice among the apostles would surely require its practice in geographically widespread congregations (e.g., Petrine and Pauline) which intentionally shared and legitimated the practice of such diversity as apostolic. Professor Lane does not seem to be arguing merely for the view that there were or may have been differences in practice in the early church period, but for a self-conscious, theologically grounded diversity in which, apparently, the choice of practice would ultimately have to reside not with the congregation as such, perhaps not even with the bishop-presbyters but (presumably?) with individuals and families. For his contention seems to be that the churches were neither credobaptist churches nor paedobaptist churches, but that they were credopaedobaptist churches.

Problems with evidence for dual practice. I see several problems with this interpretation.

1. What we find in the early theological writings are arguments about *specific* practices, not arguments for *diversity* of practices. What is lacking here is evidence of New Testament or early-century congregations that consciously and coherently adopted Professor Lane's

dual-practice position, and sought both to justify it and to practice it. Without this the theory remains just that—a theory.

2. Clearly different practices emerged in the early church. The evidence points to this not so much as a tolerated diversity of practice, but as different and indeed contrary practices. The evidence that is logically required for Professor Lane's argument to carry the day seems to me to be lacking in antiquity. The seismological probings do not take us as deeply as he would like to be able to go.

3. Furthermore this interpretation of antiquity (with its implied directive for the modern church) flies in the face of what seems to me to lie on the surface of the evidence. We do not find in the early church an enthusiasm for *diversity* so much as what seems to amount at times to a passion for a *unity* of practice bordering on uniformity. The arguments of early writers on baptism express a more totalitarian approach than a tolerated diversity interest.

In connection with the events of the day of Pentecost Dr. Lane notes, wisely,

> The New Testament church was not a student Christian Union of youngsters who had yet to settle down and have families. The three thousand converts at the day of Pentecost must have had many children of every age. Whether or not to baptize babies was an issue that had to be decided *that day*. How was it decided? (p. 144)

This, it seems to me, is a fair assessment and indeed is almost self-evidently true. What is less clear is the relationship between Professor Lane's conclusion and the decision reached by the apostles. Are we to understand that they adopted the "middle-Lane(!) position"? Was infant baptism practiced in the New Testament church but within the context of an individualized decision for each family or individual within each local congregation? The actual administration of baptism would then be a kind of "fielder's choice."

Evidence Against Early Church Dual Practice
Several things militate against this.

The sound of silence. First, no evidence for such diversity appears in the New Testament.

Professor Lane asks:

> Does not acceptance of the authority of Scripture mean respecting the silences of Scripture as well as its positive statements? The silences are there in order to leave the church liberty to vary its practice to suit different circumstances. They sanction the variety of practice that we see in the early church. (p. 166)

This view labors under an obvious difficulty. Silence per se, without further biblical-theological considerations which help to break it, can hardly act as a sanction. In this instance it is difficult to see how it can sanction a variety of practice. If there were total silence, without clues as to activity within the silence, it surely remains exactly that—silence.

Lack of appeal. Second, I find no memory of, appeal to, or critique of such dual practice after the New Testament period. Professor Lane notes the importance of appeal to the apostolic church in early theologians. He concludes that the lack of appeal to apostolic practice by an early theologian probably implies that he *could not* appeal to such practice, otherwise his failure to appeal to it would be unthinkable. Does the same argument not operate here also? If this specific form of "dual practice" were the apostolic norm (or even the postapostolic norm), surely appeal to such a practice would be found in the writings of the Fathers? But none is adduced.

Is sufficient ground negotiable? Third, if there is no theological ground for the baptism of the infants of all believers, can there be a *sufficient* ground for the baptism of any infant of any believer? Professor Lane surmises that the practice in the earliest period may have been for converts' present children to be baptized with them, while any later-born children may have been baptized at a later stage. "If this were so we would have a variety of practice already in New Testament times and this would account for the nondogmatic approach taken in the following three centuries" (p. 159).

The problem here is that the early literature does not suggest a "nondogmatic" (i.e., a nonuniform) approach, but precisely the opposite. Neither the New Testament nor later literature seems to encourage this specific kind of diversity within the local congregation. It is surely stretching the silence of the period to suggest that it mandates such an unaffirmed and radical diversity in a rite so central to the church as baptism.

Apostolic D-Day. Fourth, Professor Lane makes a key admission when he concedes (more, affirms) that a decision about the baptism of infants must have taken place no later than the day of Pentecost (see p. 181). That such a decision amounted simply to "Make up your own minds" seems inconceivable in the light of the absoluteness of the command to be baptized for the forgiveness of sins (Acts 2:38). If the apostles baptized infants (which Professor Lane holds is highly likely), would this not have constituted both apostolic doctrine and apostolic practice (and that as an expression of our Lord's authority, Mt 28:18-20)? To these twin realities the first Christians were admirably addicted (Acts 2:42). Should we not follow their example?

Three further considerations arise here, albeit on a somewhat different plane.

By what authority? Fifth, and by way of question as much as reservation, it is not clear to me on what grounds Professor Lane believes infants should be baptized, nor what he means by speaking of infant baptism as an "adaptation" of converts' baptism. The question is: What was adapted—the amount of water? The meaning? The grounds? In my own view (albeit not all paedobaptists have shared it) the rite has one and the same objective meaning when administered to converts and when administered to their infant children, even if there is diversity in its "meaningfulness" to the recipient at the moment of administration.

Common ground? Sixth, I have some reservations about the validity of an appeal to "common ground" (p. 163) in the fact that while paedobaptists baptize their children, many credobaptists will have "some sort of dedication ceremony" (p. 163). It is not so clear to me that the ground is really "common" in the sense of being neutral. Some of the arguments used by credobaptists against the baptism of infants tell also against the dedication of their own infants. There may be similar-looking practices without there actually being common ground:

- The child must make its own decision about Christ. How then can parents make it in infant dedication?

- Paedobaptists do not recognize the radical discontinuity between the old and the new covenant. But infant dedications are pre-Pentecost realities (and, interestingly, additional to circumcision!).

- How can a rite the child does not understand at the moment of administration be relevant to the child? But the dedicated child is no more conscious than the baptized one.

In effect, then, the service of infant dedication turns out either to share paedobaptist theology, but not see it through to its appropriate conclusion (i.e., to reject the common ground, even if apparently engaged in an analogous rite), or to be a dedication of the parents, not of the infant. While there is indeed a dedication on the part of parents at the baptism of an infant, *that* is not the common ground that Professor Lane is claiming.

Evangelical baptismal ecumenicity. Seventh, Dr. Lane appeals to such evangelical-ecumenical events as the British "Spring Harvest" gathering where the children of believers are taught by both credobaptists and paedobaptists without difficulty or tension. Indeed Professor Lane asks if it is not irrelevant what their view of baptism is. The implication seems to be that baptismal theology makes no (significant?) difference to the teaching, nor to the teachers. The implied conclusion would seem to be that all that is required is that this trajectory be continued into the life of the churches.

This is surely true only if baptism is, by agreement, deliberately made irrelevant in both doctrine and practice for the short duration of the event. This is possible only because of the parachurch nature of the event where, for a short period of time, in a noncongregational setting, it is possible to focus on a selected variety of themes. By contrast, over the long haul in the life of the church family and its families, it is precisely the theology that undergirds baptism that leads to the implications that flow from it in personal, family and church fellowship life.

CONCLUSION

This is not merely a matter of an abstract rite. Here I agree very much with Professor Lane's insistence that the issue is not simply the event of baptism as such (pp. 168-69). For, despite protests to the contrary, it is difficult to see how evangelicals can, *with theological consistency*, teach their children to say "Our Father" and to sing the psalms, hymns and spiritual songs with any theological consistency apart from the undergirding relationship established by God's covenant promise and the principle that they belong by covenant to the community of God's people. The question of the child's relationship to the church is vital. The fact that the articulation of it is sometimes regarded as of secondary importance should not obscure its actual importance.

Throughout the centuries the debate about baptism has generally proceeded on the presupposition *tertium non datur*—either credobaptism or paedobaptism. Professor Lane's irenic aspiration to a congregational lifestyle in which both converts' baptism and infant baptism or later profession baptism are practiced expresses an admirable desire for the visible unity of the church, a harmony of life in local congregations and for the rite of baptism not to be seen as more important than the life and worship of the baptized.

Despite the attractions of this view, however, its implementation is possible only at the price of theological reductionism and a sidelining of important pastoral questions. More fundamentally, the dual-practice hypothesis cannot point to any evidence that this style of *adiaphora* was practiced in the earliest church.

This being said, it is, I think, worth underlining that the danger of discussing baptism in a polemical context is precisely what is of special concern to Dr. Lane, namely that we endanger our common faith and repudiate a common baptism. It may also give the impression that the rite itself as an abstract reality has greater significance than it actually does. I would like therefore to conclude these comments by repeating my appreciation for Professor Lane's aspirations and goals. Baptism is a sign; it is not the reality it signifies. The gospel itself is more important than any of its signs (Gal 6:15; 1 Cor 1:16). At the end of the day, I remain convinced that the most theologically consistent "dual practice" is within well-regulated, covenant-grounded paedobaptist churches—where Professor Lane knows he will be welcomed!

Concluding Response

Anthony N. S. Lane

I AM GRATEFUL TO MY TWO COLLEAGUES for their gracious responses. I shall make some comments on these and then end with a concluding remark. I must apologize to Bruce Ware and to any readers who were likewise confused by my references to "converts' baptism." My point was not to distinguish between believers and converts as if some converts were not true believers. It was, with Beasley-Murray,[1] to make the point that in Acts we find not just that believers were baptized but that they were baptized at the point when they come to faith.

It is not just that converts are baptized, but that they are baptized on the occasion of their conversion. My point was the *simultaneity* of baptism and conversion/coming to faith. Baptism has a meaning and significance in the context of conversion that it does not so easily have for those who have already believed for many years. In particular the instrumental role of baptism, baptism as the appropriation of salvation, makes sense when those being baptized have just come to faith/been converted. Indeed baptism is itself a part of their conversion.

Bruce Ware is unhappy with my use of the historical record.

---

[1]George R. Beasley-Murray, *Baptism in the New Testament* (London: Macmillan, 1962).

Against it he appeals "with the Reformers" to the principle of *sola Scriptura*.[2] This he understands to mean that the Bible is "the only final and only absolutely authoritative source for our belief and practice as Christians" (p. 175). If that is how the principle is understood, then I gladly join him in affirming it. I am not aware that I have infringed it. I have used the evidence of the early centuries to help us to understand what happened in the apostolic church. I have not treated it as either a final or an absolutely authoritative source—and certainly do not regard it as such. He himself writes of the "historical support for believers' baptism," referring to the practice of the first four centuries. It is clear that he does not regard this practice as normative for us (any more than I do) but that he does see it as further confirmation of what he sees in the New Testament. In this subordinate role I too make use of the evidence from the first few centuries. I do make more use of it than he does, and it plays a more significant role in my argument. But I do not, any more than he, regard the practice of the patristic church as normative for us today.

Am I arguing that "variety in belief and practice [in Christian history] indicate that the church should adopt a flexible stance toward these areas"? Certainly not. My argument is that the New Testament is silent about what happened to the children of believers and that the subsequent variety in the early centuries suggests that this variety goes back to New Testament times. I am using the later variety as *historical evidence* to help us penetrate behind the silence of the New Testament record. I am appealing to the later variety not as having any authority in itself but as evidence for what might have happened in apostolic times.

I am grateful to Sinclair Ferguson for his witty and perceptive comments. How I wish I had thought first of calling my view the "middle-Lane position"! However, at a few points I was not per-

---

[2]In fact the *sola Scriptura* formula is a post-Reformation development, though the principle that it encapsulates comes from the Reformation. For its origin and meaning, see A. N. S. Lane, "Sola scriptura? Making Sense of a Post-Reformation Slogan," in *A Pathway into the Holy Scripture,* ed. P. E. Satterthwaite and D. F. Wright (Grand Rapids: Eerdmans, 1994), pp. 297-327.

suaded by his comments. He denies the existence of any evidence of "early century congregations that consciously and coherently adopted [my] dual practice position, and sought both to justify and to practice it. Without this the theory remains just that—a theory."

This demand would be hard to meet, not least because in his view any such congregation would probably by definition be acting incoherently! What we certainly do have evidence for is the fact that people were baptized at all sorts of ages in the third and fourth centuries. We know of no objections to this in principle. It is hard to be sure about specific congregations, but we do have the example of the influential church father Gregory Nazianzen, who recommends to a specific congregation baptism at age three, but clearly leaves the decision to the parents.

Maybe Sinclair Ferguson's rigorous demand is not met, but there is *clear* evidence for the variety of practice and its toleration. Dual practice is not "just theory" but the indisputable practice of these two centuries. Turning his point round, we have no specific congregation to which we can point and say that it had a uniformity of practice on this point. Certainly no evidence points to a congregation that taught that other congregations with a different practice were heretical.

Professor Ferguson objects that what we see is not "tolerated diversity of practice" but "different and indeed contrary practices." The practices are certainly different and also contrary to the extent that no individual can experience both. But it is equally true that this "diversity of practice" was tolerated. Where do we find evidence in the third or fourth century of the nontoleration of this diversity, of the attempt to impose uniformity? The most that we find is the urging of one policy over others as more expedient (Tertullian and the delay of baptism; Gregory and baptizing three-year olds), not the claim that one is right and the others are wrong.

Again it is certainly true in general that in the early church we find not "an enthusiasm for *diversity* so much as what seems to amount at times to a passion for a *unity* of practice bordering on uniformity."

Given that fact,[3] the clear toleration of diversity on our present topic is all the more remarkable. It is not derived from a liberal indifferentism. The persistence of this tolerated diversity points, I would suggest, to the fact that it was an ancient, most likely apostolic, tradition.

I argued that were the apostolic church to have uniformly baptized or not baptized babies this would have been known and those in favor of or against the practice would have appealed to this to commend their view. Sinclair Ferguson turns this argument against me, asking why the writings of the Fathers record no appeal to the apostolic origins of dual practice. My response would be that they had no need to make such an appeal since variety of practice was accepted everywhere. They do not appeal to apostolic practice on this for the same reason that they do not appeal to apostolic teaching for the use of water in baptism—no one questioned it.

Sinclair Ferguson continues that "the early literature does not suggest a 'nondogmatic' (i.e., a nonuniform) approach, but precisely the opposite." Where our present topic is concerned, I beg to differ. No evidence at all exists for "the opposite," but we do have Gregory Nazianzen, no marginal figure but the son of a bishop and himself bishop of Constantinople, precisely offering suggestions to parents as to when they might choose to have their children baptized, with no hint that there was only one single correct answer.

Reading Sinclair Ferguson's points, which mostly amount to an appeal to the move toward uniformity in the early centuries, I am all the more powerfully struck by the remarkable phenomenon that on this question, whether or not to baptize babies, we find no such uniformity but rather the acceptance of variety. So remarkable is it that it needs to be explained—and apostolic variety is the most plausible explanation. Reading his points again, I also wonder whether I have myself been guilty of imposing a limitation of variety by talking of

---

[3]Actually I think that Sinclair Ferguson exaggerates the extent of uniformity in the fourth century, to my advantage. After all, there was still no finally fixed canon of the NT, no agreed canon of the OT, no single definitive creed.

"dual practice." This implies that the early church had just two options, but the practice of the third and fourth centuries is far too varied to be reduced to merely two options! "Plural practice" would, in retrospect, have been a better term.

He also asks exactly what I am claiming for the apostolic age. Am I just stating that among the churches one could find a variety of practice? Or am I claiming that some "credopaedobaptist" congregations self-consciously embraced dual practice? This is a good question and is not explicitly answered in my essay. We need to differentiate between the first century and the fourth. For the first century I claim only that the most likely scenario is a variety of practice. Putting it negatively, it is less likely that the apostolic church was uniformly paedobaptist or credobaptist. As for how this variety took place, we can discover no clear evidence. I did offer some tentative suggestions: "We have already proposed the difference between babies born before and after their parents' baptism. Another option would be different policies for Jews, who circumcised their children, and Gentiles who did not. It is also possible that variety was introduced as the church spread into different places." When it comes to the fourth century, we have Gregory's sermon, which does indicate parental choice. My thesis does not depend on there being parental choice on the day of Pentecost or at any other point in New Testament history. It is simply that if there was variety of practice in the apostolic church (for *whatever* reason[s]), that is sufficient ground to question the exclusive hegemonistic claims made by paedobaptists and credobaptists alike.

The charge that my view is "just theory" is a serious one. Bruce Ware also describes it as "fully unrealistic," "something of a utopian vision," lacking "practical viability." We know that consistent and dogmatic paedobaptism has been practiced since the fifth century, and consistent and dogmatic credobaptism since the sixteenth century. When and where has "dual/plural practice," the "middle-Lane position" been put into practice? Certainly in the third and fourth centuries, the earliest centuries for which we have clear evidence.

Increasingly today. This is partly because of ecumenical ventures
which deliberately embrace both practices within the same congregation. It is also happening increasingly in a number of paedobaptist
denominations,[4] where many committed Christians choose not to
have their children baptized as babies. In such a setting "dual practice" is now widely practiced, and a service of dedication is offered
to parents as an alternative to paedobaptism. While this may have
been originally intended for use by nonchurchgoing families, it is
widely used today by committed Christians who do not wish to have
their babies baptized. Thus in many evangelical congregations parents make the choice—as in the Evangelical Covenant denomination described by Bruce Ware.

Finally, a concluding comment. Sinclair Ferguson, in his response
to Bruce Ware, rightly notes that they differ in their understanding
of what baptism is. For the one it is primarily a sign of what we receive from Christ; for the other it is a sign of our faith and an act of
obedience/commitment. For me baptism (together with faith and in
a subordinate role) is primarily an instrument by which we embrace
Christ and his salvation. It is not that the points made by the other
two are untrue but that they are not where the emphasis of the New
Testament teaching on baptism lies. In the New Testament baptism
above all *receives* Christ and his salvation. Along the way it is also a
sign both of that salvation and of our faith, but neither of these points
is developed by the New Testament writers.

---

[4]E.g., Church of England.

CONTRIBUTORS

Sinclair B. Ferguson is senior minister at First Presbyterian Church, Columbia, South Carolina, and professor of systematic theology at Redeemer Seminary, Dallas, Texas. Among his many books are *The Holy Spirit*, *John Owen on the Christian Life* and *The Christian Life: A Doctrinal Introduction*.

Anthony N. S. Lane is professor of historical theology at London School of Theology, Northwood, England. He is the author of several books, including *John Calvin: Student of the Church Fathers* and *Justification by Faith in Catholic-Protestant Dialogue: An Evangelical Assessment*.

Daniel G. Reid is a senior editor for reference and academic books at IVP Academic.

Bruce A. Ware is professor of Christian theology at The Southern Baptist Theological Seminary, Louisville, Kentucky. He is the author of several books, including *God's Greater Glory: The Exalted God of Scripture and the Christian Faith* and *Father, Son, and Holy Spirit: Relationships, Roles, and Relevance*.

David F. Wright (1937-2008) was professor of patristic and Reformation Christianity at New College, University of Edinburgh, Scotland. Among his many published studies on historical and theological topics are several on baptism, including *What Has Infant Baptism Done to Baptism? An Enquiry at the End of Christendom*.

A BIBLIOGRAPHY OF
DAVID F. WRIGHT'S
PUBLICATIONS ON BAPTISM

Baptism, Eucharist & Ministry (the 'Lima Report'): an Evangelical Assessment. Rutherford Forum Papers 3. Edinburgh: Rutherford House, 1984.

"The Lima Report: *Baptism* and *Eucharist* Compared." *Theology* 87 (1984): 330-36.

"The Origins of Infant Baptism—Child Believers' Baptism?" *Scottish Journal of Theology* 40 (1987): 1-23.

"How Controversial Was the Development of Infant Baptism in the Early Church?" In *Church, Word and Spirit: Historical and Theological Essays in Honor of Geoffrey W. Bromiley,* edited by James E. Bradley and Richard A. Muller, pp. 45-63. Grand Rapids: Eerdmans, 1987.

"Donatist Theologoumena in Augustine? Baptism, Reviviscence of Sins, and Unworthy Ministers." In *Congresso Internazionale su S. Agostino nel XVI Centenario della Conversione. Atti II* Studia Ephemerides "Augustinianum" 25, pp. 213-24. Rome: Institutum Patristicum "Augustinianum," 1987.

"One Baptism or Two? Reflections on the History of Christian Baptism." *Vox Evangelica* 18 (1988): 7-23 [1987 Laing Lecture].

"The Meaning and Reference of 'One Baptism for the Remission of Sins' in the Niceno-Constantinopolitan Creed." In *Studia Patristica* 19, edited by

E. A. Livingstone, pp. 281-85. Leuven: Peeters, 1989 [Tenth International Conference on Patristic Studies].

"George Cassander and the Appeal to the Fathers in Sixteenth-Century Debates about Infant Baptism." In *Auctoritas Patrum. Contributions on the Reception of the Church Fathers in the 15th and 16th Century,* edited by L. Grane, A. Schindler and M. Wriedt, pp. 259-69. Veröffentlichungen des Instituts für Europäische Geschichte Mainz 37. Abteilung Religionsgeschichte. Mainz: Philipp von Zabern, 1993.

"Baptism." In *Dictionary of Scottish Church History and Theology,* edited by N. M. de S. Cameron, pp. 56-58. Edinburgh: T & T Clark, 1993.

"Infant Baptism and the Christian Community in Bucer." In *Martin Bucer, Reforming Church and Community,* edited by David F. Wright, pp. 95-106. Cambridge: Cambridge University Press, 1994.

"Scripture and Evangelical Diversity with Special Reference to the Baptismal Divide." In *A Pathway into the Holy Scripture,* edited by David F. Wright and Philip E. Satterthwaite, pp. 257-75. Grand Rapids: Eerdmans, 1994.

"Recovering Baptism for a New Age of Mission." In *Doing Theology for the People of God: Studies in Honor of J. I. Packer,* edited by Donald Lewis and Alister McGrath, pp. 51-66. Downers Grove, Ill.: InterVarsity Press, 1996.

"Baptism at the Westminster Assembly." In *The Westminster Confession in Current Thought,* edited by J. H. Leith, pp. 76-90. Calvin Studies 8. Davidson, N.C.: Davidson College, 1996.

"At What Ages Were People Baptized in the Early Centuries? A Quest for Statistics." *Studia Patristica* 30, pp. 389-94. Leuven: Peeters, 1997. [Twelfth International Conference on Patristic Studies].

"Monnica's Baptism, Augustine's Deferred Baptism, and Patricius." *Augustinian Studies* 29, no. 2 (1998): 1-17.

"The Donatists in the Sixteenth Century." In *Auctoritas Patrum II. New Contributions on the Reception of the Church Fathers in the 15th and 16th Centuries,* edited by Leif Grane, Alfred Schindler and Markus Wriedt, pp. 281-93. Veröffentlichungen des Instituts für Europäische Geschichte Mainz 44.

Abteilung abendländische Religionsgeschichte. Edited by Gerhard May. Mainz: Philipp von Zabern, 1998.

"Infant Dedication in the Early Church." In *Baptism, the New Testament and the Church,* edited by Stanley E. Porter and A. R. Cross, pp. 352-78. Sheffield, U.K.: Sheffield Academic Press, 1999.

"1 Corinthians 7:14 in Fathers and Reformers." In *Die Patristik in der Bibelexegese des 16. Jahrhunderts,* edited by D. C. Steinmetz, pp. 93-113. Wolfenbütteler Forschungen 85. Wiesbaden: Harrassowitz, 1999.

"Habitats of Infant Baptism." In *Theology in the Service of the Church: Essays in Honor of Thomas W. Gillespie,* edited by Wallace M. Alston, pp. 254-65. Grand Rapids and Cambridge: Eerdmans, 2000.

"Augustine and the Transformation of Baptism." In *The Origins of Christendom in the West,* edited by Alan Kreider, pp. 287-310. New York: T & T Clark, 2001.

"Out, In, Out: Jesus' Blessing of the Children and Infant Baptism." In *Dimensions of Baptism,* edited by S. E. Porter and A. R. Cross, pp. 188-206. London: Sheffield Academic Press, 2002.

"The Baptismal Community," *Bibliotheca Sacra* 160 (2003): 3-12 [2002 W. H. Griffith Thomas Lectures at Dallas Theological Seminary].

What Has Infant Baptism Done to Baptism? An Enquiry at the End of Christendom. Carlisle, U.K.: Paternoster, 2005 [2003 Didsbury Lectures].

"The Apostolic Fathers and Infant Baptism: Any Advance on the Obscurity of the New Testament?" In *Trajectories Through the New Testament and the Apostolic Fathers,* ed. A. F. Gregory and C. M. Tuckett, pp. 123-33. Oxford: Oxford University Press, 2005.

"Development and Coherence in Calvin's *Institutes:* The Case of Baptism (*Institutes* 4:15-4:16)." In *Adaptations of Calvinism in Reformation Europe: Essays in Honour of Brian G. Armstrong,* edited by M. Holt, pp. 43-54. Aldershot: Ashgate, 2006.

Scripture Index